THE REAL READER'S QUARTERLY

Slightly Foxed

'Adrift on the Tides of War'

NO.63   AUTUMN 2019

Editors Gail Pirkis & Hazel Wood
Marketing and publicity Stephanie Allen & Jennie Harrison Bunning
Bookshops Anna Kirk
Subscriptions Hattie Summers & Jess Dalby

Cover illustration: Louise O'Hara, 'Wandering by the Light of the Moon', mixed media

Louise O'Hara is a professional mixed media artist based in the heart of Cheshire. Her style has been described as quintessentially English, romantic and nostalgic. The work she produces is influenced by tactile aged surfaces such as peeling paint on walls and fabrics that are threadbare but which are laden with memories. For more of her work and to contact her see her website (www.louiseohara.co.uk) or follow her on Instagram (@louiseoharaart) or Pinterest (@louiseOHaraArt/my-work).

Design by Octavius Murray
Layout by Andrew Evans
Colophon and tailpiece by David Eccles

Published by Slightly Foxed Limited
53 Hoxton Square
London N1 6PB

tel 020 7033 0258
email office@foxedquarterly.com
www.foxedquarterly.com

Slightly Foxed is published quarterly in early March, June, September and December

Annual subscription rates (4 issues)
UK and Ireland £48; Overseas £56

Single copies of this issue can be bought for £12.50 (UK) or £14.50 (Overseas)

All back issues in printed form are also available

ISBN 978-1-910898-34-5
ISSN 1742-5794

Printed and bound by Smith Settle, Yeadon, West Yorkshire

Contents

From the Editors   5

Adrift on the Tides of War · PATRICK WELLAND
Olivia Manning's Balkan trilogy   7

Hands off the Handlebars · SUE GEE
Roald Dahl, *Boy*   15

One of the Regulars · LINDA LEATHERBARROW
Penelope Fitzgerald, *The Means of Escape*   21

'Tis Better to Have Loved and Lost? · CHRISTOPHER RUSH
Alfred, Lord Tennyson, *In Memoriam*   26

The Sound of Chariots · SUE GAISFORD
The Roman Britain novels of Rosemary Sutcliff   33

Porridge and the Shorter Catechism · MORAG MCINNES
F. M. McNeill, *The Scots Kitchen*   40

Challenging the Old Gang · MICHAEL BARBER
Noel Annan, *Our Age*   44

Hauntings · MICHÈLE ROBERTS
Dorothy L. Sayers, *Gaudy Night*   49

Hitting the Nail on the Head · YSENDA MAXTONE GRAHAM
The poetry of Jan Struther   55

The Twilight Hour · MIRANDA SEYMOUR
Peter Davidson, *The Last of the Light*   63

Contents

At War with Churchill · ANTHONY LONGDEN
Field Marshal Lord Alanbrooke, *War Diaries*   69

Lost in the Fens · JULIE WELCH
The detective stories of Edmund Crispin   77

Winning on Points · JACQUELINE WILSON
Noel Streatfeild, *Ballet Shoes*   83

Word Magic · TIM MACKINTOSH-SMITH
Becoming a writer   89

Bibliography   94

John Watson

The Slightly Foxed Podcast

The first ten episodes of our new podcast are now available. To listen, visit www.foxedquarterly.com/pod or search for Slightly Foxed on Audioboom, iTunes or your podcast app. Future episodes will be available on the 15th of each month.

Subscriber Benefits

Slightly Foxed can obtain any books reviewed in this issue, whether new or second-hand. To enquire about a book, to access the digital edition of *Slightly Foxed* or to view a list of membership benefits, visit www.foxedquarterly.com/members or contact the office: 020 7033 0258/office@foxedquarterly.com.

From the Editors

September has crept up on us; it won't be long before we're thinking about Christmas (our new festive foxed card, the fifth in the series, is now out) and here in the office there's that familiar, excited beginning-of-term feeling of things about to happen.

One of them is certainly the appearance this autumn of two new titles in the Cubs series. They are the first two books in a quartet of novels set in Roman Britain by one of the greatest children's writers, Rosemary Sutcliff, whose memoir of her early life, *Blue Remembered Hills*, we published in 2008 as the first of our Slightly Foxed Editions.

Sutcliff was a most interesting person. Diagnosed when she was very young with a form of juvenile arthritis that left her severely disabled and prevented her going to school (she didn't learn to read until she was 9), she nevertheless became a talented painter of miniatures before truly finding herself as a children's author. She never married, but in her early twenties, shortly before she began to write, she suffered the agony of rejection by a man she was seriously in love with, and perhaps this accounts for some of the imaginative intensity she poured into her work, especially into the four outstanding novels that chronicle the Roman occupation of Britain. We are reissuing all four in hand-numbered limited editions of 2,000 copies each. *The Eagle of the Ninth* and *The Silver Branch* (see p.33) are available now, and *Frontier Wolf* and *The Lantern Bearers* will be published in September 2020 but can be pre-ordered now. We loved these books as children, and they were just as gripping the second time round.

The same applies to *Boy*, by another brilliant storyteller, Roald Dahl, the latest of the Slightly Foxed Editions (see p.15). The language of this childhood memoir is simple, but goodness how it grabs you. It's a story peopled by many of the real-life ogres who later in one guise or another crept into Dahl's fiction – brutal headmasters, grim-faced matrons, bullying prefects and a vengeful sweet-shop owner – but counterbalancing this is his relationship with his adored mother and the idyllic summers the family spent among the fjords of her native Norway. An absolute treat and not to be missed.

Good news too for anyone who missed out on two of our bestselling SFEs, Helene Hanff's *84, Charing Cross Road* and *Corduroy*, the first book in Adrian Bell's Suffolk farming trilogy: both are now available as Plain Foxed editions. And there are still a few copies left of *A Country Doctor's Commonplace Book*, the perfect Christmas present for anyone – and this probably includes most of us these days – badly in need of a laugh.

All this talk of new books leads us to the tricky subject of marketing. Most of the letters we receive from you are cheeringly positive, but a few of you, we know, feel that you sometimes receive too many postal and online communications from us.

As you can imagine, the life of a small independent business like ours is pleasurable but not easy. We have no big financial backers: our shareholders are members of staff and friends who put their money and trust in us at the beginning. We promised then that we would provide readers with a personal service, that anyone who phoned us would be answered by a human being, that we would try to maintain the highest editorial and production standards, and treat our suppliers and contributors well, and we hope we've kept that promise.

We know you appreciate this, but it does come at a cost and one that's ever rising. So we do our best to tread the fine line between maximizing our business and keeping you up-to-date while not being too intrusive. We truly value your opinions and listen to what you say. So if you do have thoughts on the subject of marketing, of whatever kind, do please share them with us.

GAIL PIRKIS & HAZEL WOOD

Adrift on the Tides of War

PATRICK WELLAND

It is an irony that the dramatization of a novel may deter not spur. Instead of leading the viewer to the book, it becomes a substitute. Such a fate appears to have befallen Olivia Manning's *Fortunes of War*, which in its Balkan and Levant trilogies traces the wartime travails of young Harriet and Guy Pringle as they flee the advancing Germans, first in Bucharest and Athens, then in Egypt and the Middle East. The six volumes were published to acclaim between 1960 and 1980. Yet Manning's work is now probably better remembered as the 1987 BBC TV dramatization starring Emma Thompson and Kenneth Branagh.

This is unjust. *Fortunes* is a triumph, fusing fiction with diligently researched fact to portray a disparate group of expatriates surviving under threat of invasion: their stoicism, heroism and cowardice; their fleeting romances and petty intrigues. The prose is economical and the gaze sceptical and unsentimental. Added to this tapestry is a rich evocation of contemporary society, place and manners. Anthony Burgess called the sequence the 'finest fictional record of the war produced by a British writer'.

Fortunes is unashamedly autobiographical, a creative reconstruction of actual people and events, with the fictionalized emotional battleground of Manning's marriage to the ebullient Reggie Smith mirroring the wider conflict.

Olivia Manning's Balkan trilogy, *The Great Fortune* (1960), *The Spoilt City* (1962) and *Friends and Heroes* (1965), is available in a single-volume paperback: Arrow · 1,040pp · £18.99 · ISBN 9780099427483.

I was drawn to the series because my father served in wartime Greece and Egypt, and I thought I might glimpse some part of his experience about which, like so many veterans, he was reticent. I was also intrigued to read, from the perspective of a sharp and critical intelligence, how a generation raised to believe in the certainties of empire reacted to the disillusion occasioned when those certainties were found wanting.

Manning's literary achievement is the greater for the obstacles she faced. Born in Portsmouth in 1908, she had no educational or social privileges. Her naval officer father was easy-going and warm-hearted. Her mother, the daughter of an Ulster Presbyterian publican, was a

rancorous termagant who hen-pecked her husband and turned against her daughter when her son was born. Money was short and rows were frequent. Yet, remarkably, this effectively self-educated woman fought her way into the literary world. In her mid-20s she moved to London, took ill-paid temping jobs and wrote in every spare moment. Her first novel was published in 1937. She remained, however, blighted by a sense of inferiority which literary success could assuage but not dispel. Nicknamed Olivia Moaning, she could be prickly in company and frequently complained that she did not receive due credit.

Manning, then 31, met Reggie, six years younger, in London in 1939. He was everything she was not – open-hearted, charismatic and a committed Communist. Reggie had transcended his working-class background to graduate with honours in English, which he was then teaching at the British Council in Bucharest. Olivia was socially awkward and haunted by sour provincial memories. Yet only three weeks after being introduced, they married.

Five days later Reggie returned to Bucharest with his bride, arriving on the Orient Express on 3 September, the day Britain declared war on Germany. The Balkan trilogy's first book, *The Great Fortune*, opens with Harriet and Guy – here, 22 and 23 – making the same journey. The seizure by officials of a German-Jewish refugee who has lost his documents, the 'dark heart of the forest' through which they travel and the reflected eyes of beasts flitting through the night-time woods presage the uncertainty and menace to come.

Guy, like Reggie, is teaching at the British Council. Harriet, unlike her creator who wrote continuously during her years in wartime exile, has no moorings other than her husband whose love she desires as a bulwark against the world. The alienation and dislocation which result from the discovery that Guy prefers to embrace the society of others reflect Manning's own emotional and physical experience.

In late 1939, neutral Romania is in denial. Germany is poised like a vulture, waiting to feast on a nation corrupted by social inequality and political dissension. Yet in Bucharest the orchestras play on in the packed cafés and garden restaurants, crowds still clog the pavements in the traditional evening parade, shops are stocked with luxury foods and clothes. The mutilated beggars and peasants squatting beside their meagre wares make a disagreeable contrast to this brittle display of complacency. But no one has ever cared about them.

Days after the Pringles arrive, the Prime Minister is shot by the fascist Iron Guard on German instructions. Meanwhile, a propaganda war breaks out between the British and German information bureaux on opposite sides of the Calea Victoriei. The English gather in the English Bar of the Athénée Palace Hotel. The German diplomats and staff base themselves in the nearby Minerva Hotel.

Under this gathering storm, the embattled English colony of Council staff, diplomats, university teachers and seedy journalists nervously waits upon events. Some, like Guy and his chief, Inchcape, are determined to see matters through to the end, hopelessly waving the flag. Others such as the insufferable lecturer Lord Pinkrose look only to their own safety. The Romanians hold the British in increasing contempt as it becomes clear that Germany is in the ascendant.

Rising above them all is one of the great fictional creations of the twentieth century, the splendidly inglorious figure of Prince Yakimov, apparently based on the louche Fitzrovian Julian Maclaren-Ross. Half Anglo-Irish and half White Russian, the former playboy arrives in Bucharest unwashed and starving. Trailing his tatty, sable-lined coat which 'the Czar gave to m'poor old dad, you know', this shameless sponger moves through the trilogy, attaching himself to whoever will buy him a drink or a meal while living on memories of his once gilded life and yearning for his abandoned Hispano-Suiza. Through his eyes we witness the rotten heart of the Bucharest bourgeoisie when he is grudgingly admitted to its company, and the poverty of its backstreets where he is forced to find lodgings. His greed and amorality invite our disdain. Yet as he infuriates so he charms, finally achieving a dubious dignity.

Harriet, nervous and shy, soon realizes that she cannot rely on her husband to guide her through this unsettling world. Warm-hearted and gregarious, Guy indiscriminately embraces all he meets, inspiring devotion and loyalty. But as he is open to the cares of others so he is blind to Harriet's needs. 'She had, in all innocence, been prepared to possess him and be possessed in a relationship that excluded the enemy world . . . Guy was not playing his part. Through him the world was not only admitted, but welcomed.'

As Harriet makes her way in this society, she befriends the lively Bella, an Englishwoman married to a Romanian, and embarks on a chaste affair with the cynical and vapid Clarence Lawson who is working for the Propaganda Bureau. Meanwhile, the mood of imminent disaster deepens. Emmanuel Drucker, a wealthy Jewish banker, is arrested on trumped-up charges and vanishes into the prison system. Menacing Iron Guard youths, their faces scarred like German duellists, appear on the streets. Their day is soon to come.

France is invaded and the German residents become increasingly cocky, taking over the English Bar in the Athénée Palace. Paris falls and the map in the German Bureau now shows the French capital 'hidden by a swastika that squatted like a spider, black on the heart of the country'. Romania itself, with its rich natural resources now so eagerly demanded by Germany, was once itself the 'Great Fortune'. Now Harriet declares: 'The great fortune is life. We must preserve it.'

The twin themes of societal and marital disintegration increase in intensity in the second book of the trilogy, *The Spoilt City*. Bucharest, crowded with refugees, bakes in a dry and dusty heat, its shrivelled parks, closed cafés and weed-strewn lakes mirroring its inner decay. King Carol, aware that England is powerless to help, declares for the Axis. Fears that Britain is now too weak to resist the jackboot are confirmed when the British Bureau is ransacked and Inchcape is brutally beaten by unknown assailants.

Horrors lurk beneath the surface of everyday life and rumours abound that thousands have been arrested or executed. The fate of the Jews is captured in a final sighting of the arrested banker Drucker. Harriet last met the elegant patriarch and his family living in a cocoon of false security, believing their wealth would shield them from persecution. Now, ten months after his seizure, she witnesses his departure from court:

> What appeared was an elderly, stooping skeleton   he paused and one of the warders gave him a kick that sent him sprawling over the pavement. As he picked himself up there came from him a stench like the stench of a carrion bird. The warder kicked at him again and he fell forward clutching at the van steps and murmuring 'da, da' in zealous obedience.

It is enough. We know too well what is to come.

And what of the egregious Yakimov in these perilous times? Sensing what is in the wind, 'your poor old Yaki' tops greed and cowardice with treason by seeking sanctuary in Transylvania where Freddie von Flugel, an old friend from pre-war society days, is the Nazi Gauleiter. Outrageously, he presents him with a British sabotage plan he has stolen and implicates Guy.

Throughout the trilogy it is hard to gauge where fact ends and fiction begins, with elements of a *roman à clef* enfolded in the leisurely embrace of a *roman fleuve*. Typical is the arrival in Bucharest in September 1940 of the outriders of a German delegation after Romania and Germany have signed a pact. Harriet notes how the appearance of elegant German officers makes an erotic impression on watching women. The acuity of observation could only come from Manning's own direct experience:

> Most gazed spellbound at these desirable young men who were the more piquantly desirable because they had so recently been the enemy. When the Germans passed out of sight the women fell together in ecstatic appreciation, their eyes agleam, their sensuality heightened by the proximity of these conquerors of the world.

It is a moment indicative of the fatal weakness lying at the heart of a country so corrupted from within that it welcomes the predators who will rape it of its resources and drag it into war.

Later, the Pringles and the odious Lord Pinkrose find themselves attending by mistake a German propaganda concert where they stand for 'Deutschland über Alles' before leaving in humiliation as the 'Horst Wessel' song blares out. When Harriet and Guy return from a break to find their flat raided and Drucker's gentle son Sasha – whom they have been hiding – gone, it is clear time has run out. Harriet grudgingly agrees to catch a flight to Athens, leaving Guy to join her later.

Manning, drained by the tensions of Bucharest, made the same fraught journey and her relief at arriving in the 'longed-for city' is reflected in the early chapters of the final book in the trilogy, *Friends and Heroes*. Reunited with Guy, Harriet revels in the contrast between a country that has sold itself in fear and a welcoming people at ease with themselves. Here, the expats are not resident through the necessity of work but because they choose to live in a country they love. And 'here one had only to be English to be approved'.

Greek affection for the English reaches new heights after Greece repels Mussolini's forces on the Albanian border in a string of successes that have jubilant Athenians surging on to the streets. In response, Britain establishes military bases in the country and its newly arrived young servicemen, 'pink-faced and sheepish', are greeted with flowers, hugs and cheers.

The Pringles, warmed by the Aegean sun and the kindness of the local populace, are released from the threatening claustrophobia that poisoned Bucharest. Harriet is also released from her emotional dependency on Guy. While her husband is demoralized by his temporary unemployment, Harriet comes to accept the incompatibilities in their marriage and emerges from his shadow. Increasingly independent, she nearly submits to the insistent courtship of a young officer, Charles Warden (based on the Council lecturer Terence Spencer with whom Manning may have had an affair).

As in Bucharest, the threat of German invasion is always implicit, and Manning explores the gradual erosion of spirit that overtakes those living in constant tension: the clutch of Englishwomen, personified by the formidable Mrs Brett, who have chosen to stay in Athens, desperately trying to keep up appearances; the gentle Hellenophile Alan Frewen – modelled on the novelist and poet Robert Liddell – determined to remain with the people he loves; the disagreeable intrigues of Council staff ruled by their unpleasant chief, Gracey, a reflection of Manning's own dislike of the organization for what she considered to be its offhand treatment of Reggie.

Familiar faces return. Lord Pinkrose, who fled Budapest in a fit of cowardice, reappears elevated to the post of Director of the English School. Tatty as ever, Yakimov has somehow found his way to Athens where he makes an uncertain living working for the British Information Bureau. This once grand figure of unapologetic self-interest is no longer trying to rise above events, instead submitting to the changing tide of fortune.

But as much as *Friends* is about the fraying of a community and the collapse of a relationship it is also about the collapse of a nation, not from inner corruption and collusion, as in Romania, but from exhaustion and overwhelming odds.

As the tide of war turns in the Germans' favour, wounded Greek troops appear in the streets, their feet wrapped in rags. Food becomes increasingly scarce. Air raids pound the capital. English troops who shortly before had driven out of Athens singing, laughing and catching flowers thrown by well-wishers, now return exhausted, carrying with them the odour of defeat. Manning's biographer Deidre David has suggested that Olivia lived with the scars of those anxious days for the rest of her life.

For the British enclave, escape is imperative. As the Pringles pack for their journey aboard the refugee ship *Erebus*, Harriet has an emotional epiphany. Looking at Guy, exhausted and for once indecisive, she realizes that for all his welcoming bonhomie he is as scared and confused as she. More importantly, she recognizes that at heart he loves her. His affection may be imperfectly displayed but it is real. 'They had learnt each other's faults and weaknesses: they had passed both illusion and disillusion. It was no use asking for more than anyone could give. War had forced their understanding . . . she had chosen to make her life with Guy and would stand by her choice.'

The *Erebus* enters Egyptian waters and the trilogy closes with a nod to the original motif of the Great Fortune: 'Still, they had life – a depleted fortune, but a fortune. They were together and would remain together, and that was the only certainty left to them.'

An article on Olivia Manning's Levant trilogy will follow in Issue 64.

PATRICK WELLAND is a freelance writer. He marvels at the stoicism and sense of duty displayed by his parents' wartime generation and gloomily contemplates how he would have matched up.

Hands off the Handlebars

SUE GEE

Walking home one afternoon from Llandaff Cathedral School at the age of 7, Roald Dahl was stopped in his tracks by the most tremendous sight. With his hands casually folded across his chest, a senior boy of 12 was hurtling downhill on his bike.

> I promise you that if somebody had caught me by the shoulder at that moment and said to me, 'What is your greatest ambition in life, little boy?'. . . I would have answered without hesitation that my only ambition, my hope, my longing was to have a bike like that and go whizzing down the hill with no hands on the handlebars. It would be fabulous. It made me tremble just to think about it.

By the time Dahl came to write *Boy* (1984), he was 68. Behind him was a life not without its thrilling aspects: magnificent wartime activity with the RAF in North Africa and Greece, secret intelligence work thereafter, and a famously shut-away writing life which had long since made him one of the greatest and best-loved children's authors of the twentieth century. Now he sat down to record his own childhood.

'An autobiography is a book a person writes about his own life, and it is usually full of all sorts of boring details . . .' Thus he prefaces this utterly engaging recollection of schooldays and holidays. It is, of course, full of mesmerizing details, often relating to adult whiskers, moustaches and bosoms, not to mention exploits, adventures and fun. The tone is confiding, the prose springy. And a glorious great gust of Get-up-and-get-on-with-it blows through the book, not unlike the wind in the ears of that bold young cyclist, speeding so confidently and inspiringly downhill. This spirit – and the child Dahl was nothing if not spirited – is, however, interlaced with stories of sadism, pure and simple.

Throughout his work – *James and the Giant Peach* (1961), *Charlie and the Chocolate Factory* (1964), *Fantastic Mr Fox* (1970), *Danny, The Champion of the World* (1975), *The Twits* (1980), *The BFG* (1982) and more – Dahl is firmly on the side of the child, whose world is generally populated by adult grotesques, full of cruelty, unkindness and absurd demands. In *Boy*, we can see where these creatures come from.

At Llandaff Cathedral School the boys called frequently at the local sweet shop – 'the very centre of our lives' – on the way home. A sweet shop should be presided over by a large, jolly person, but herein stands the evil Mrs Pratchett, 'a small skinny hag with a moustache on her upper lip and a mouth as sour as a green gooseberry'. Unsmiling, unwelcoming, with filthy old fingers delving into the Humbugs or Treacle Toffees, she is loathed by all her customers, and it is Dahl who hits on the idea of revenge with the Great Mouse Plot.

A wickedly splendid idea (think mouse, think sweet jar), it ends in terror and a brutal caning. It is Dahl's mother, appalled at the sight of her son's bruised bottom at bath-time, who marches off to the school to confront the headmaster. 'They don't beat small children like that where I come from,' she told him, and was told that she was a foreigner, who didn't understand how British schools were run.

Roald Dahl, born and brought up in Wales, was the son of Norwegian parents, and it is Norway, his family, his home life and above all his formidable and marvellous mother which in *Boy* provide the great contrasts with cruelty, the anchors of happiness and love.

Sofie Magdalene was the second wife of Harald Dahl, who had lost an arm in an accident and made nothing whatsoever of this disability. An entrepreneur, a lover of good things, he had set sail from Norway to Cardiff in the 1890s and founded a hugely successful shipbroking business. His first wife had died, leaving two children, Sofie Magdalene bore him five more: Roald, in 1916, and four flaxen-haired daughters, one of whom died of peritonitis at the age of 7. This broke Harald's heart, and he himself died of pneumonia not long afterwards.

Thus Sofie, at the age of 35, found herself a widow with six children to bring up and (through a trust fund) support. She made a magnificent job of it.

Dear Mama, A man called Mr Mitchell gave us a fine lecture last knight on birds . . .

Dear Mama, The wart on my thum has come off beautifly . . .

The letters home began when in 1925 the 9 year old Dahl was left with his brand-new trunk and brand-new tuck-box on the vast gravelled drive of St Peter's, Weston-super-Mare, his next school, and was flashed a shark-like grin by the headmaster. Unsurprisingly, he began to cry. In the long homesick years that followed, the letters, even though censored, were a lifeline. He was to go on writing to his mother for the rest of her life, and she kept every single one of those scrawly pages.

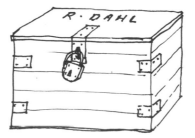

And every summer she took all the children and Nanny over to Norway to see their grandparents, Bestepapa and Bestemama. These were idyllic holidays: the lunch of freshly caught fish; the clinking of glasses of liqueur with everyone at the table; the long hot days sailing over a glassy fjord to their island retreat where they fished and swam and grew strong and fit. 'I tell you, my friends, those were the days.'

Once these summers were over, what else made his time at St Peter's bearable? The tuck-box. Ah, the tuck-box. I can remember my own mother stuffing my brother's (D.W. GEE, E16, black-painted on side and top) with flapjacks and date crunchies as he set off each term in the 1950s for his own version of prep-school hell. Like Dahl, he was hungry for years: 'an average tuck-box would probably contain, at almost any time, half a home-made currant cake, a packet of  squashed fly biscuits, a couple of oranges . . .' As in Ratty's picnic in *The Wind in the Willows*, the list goes on and on, itemizing not only food but the boys' essentials of magnet, compass, pocket knife and stink bombs – 'and I remember one boy called Arkle who drilled an airhole in the lid . . . and kept a pet frog in there which he fed on slugs'.

It is also the loyalty and friendship between the boys themselves, truly up against it, which enable them to survive this school. You might think that Matron would be a beneficent presence in such a place, and certainly my Aunt Alice, who briefly had this role before the war, adored her charges. Not so at St Peter's: 'Her age was probably no more than twenty-eight but it made no difference whether she was twenty-eight or sixty-eight because to us a grown-up was a grown-up and all grown-ups were dangerous creatures at this school.'

Dangers included the savage canings meted out for misdemeanours such as whispering in prep to your neighbour that you needed a new pen nib, and anything at all involving illness or medicine. In the 1920s, anaesthetic was not exactly unheard of, but nor was it widely used. Time in the San was time to be dreaded, and the account of little Ellis and his lanced boil is unlikely to be forgotten.

When Dahl was 13, he was sent to Repton. Here, where you wore a uniform to rival Eton's, danger came not only from the masters (more caning) but from the prefects, or Boazers (yet more). He had entered the world of fagging, where you spent icy winter mornings warming up your own particular Boazer's lavatory seat before he deposited his own rear end upon it. Dahl got through this by reading Dickens.

And he got through the whole of his time at Repton by excelling at sport, particularly squash, football and fives; because of this his life there 'was not totally without pleasure'. Though normally such an athlete would automatically have been made a Boazer, he was relieved not to be considered the right material: 'I would have let down the whole principle of Boazerdom by refusing to beat the Fags.' He also discovered photography, befriended by a quietly civilized arts master, and through days in the dark room became proficient. And in his last term he discovered something else: the joy of the motorbike, a Christmas present from his mother in 1932.

> I kept it secretly in a garage about two miles away. On Sundays I used to walk to the garage and disguise myself in helmet, goggles, old raincoat and rubber waders and ride all over Derbyshire. It was fun to go roaring through Repton itself with nobody knowing who you were, swishing past the masters . . . and the dangerous supercilious School Boazers out for their Sunday strolls.

On the last day of his last term at Repton, he mounted his motorbike and 'zoomed joyfully away and left school for ever and ever. I was not quite eighteen.'

The spirited boy had become a terrific young man: after a spell in Newfoundland with the Public Schools' Explorers, Dahl was 'hard and fit and ready for anything'. And would he, his mother now asked him, prefer to go to Oxford or Cambridge? The answer was neither: life and adventure were the thing. To find them he joined Shell, and after two years of commuting to Head Office in London, and selling kerosene to nice old ladies in sleepy Somerset, he set off for his first posting. 'I was twenty years old. I was off to East Africa where I would walk about in khaki shorts every day and wear a topi on my head! I was ecstatic.'

Life without handlebars had begun.

SUE GEE is at work on *The Wellspring of Their Art*, essay-portraits of eleven writers in different genres, to be published by Seren next year.

Roald Dahl's *Boy* (184pp) is now available in a limited and numbered cloth-bound edition of 2,000 copies (subscribers: UK & Eire £17, Overseas £19; non-subscribers: UK & Eire £18.50, Overseas £20.50). All prices include post and packing. Copies may be ordered by post (53 Hoxton Square, London N1 6PB), by phone (020 7033 0258) or via our website www.foxedquarterly.com.

This November we will also be reissuing Roald Dahl's *Going Solo*, in which he writes about his experiences in East Africa and his astonishing exploits as a fighter pilot during the Second World War. Copies can be pre-ordered now by phone or via the website.

One of the Regulars

LINDA LEATHERBARROW

At the back of Penelope Fitzgerald's only short-story collection, *The Means of Escape* (2000), there is a charming black-and-white photograph of the author. It shows her buttoned into a high-collared shirt under a garment that appears to be an academic robe but could simply be a very large cardigan. Not quite smiling, she looks gentle yet distinguished, exactly as I remember her; and, as I looked at the photograph, there she was again and so was I, back in the old public library at the top of Highgate Hill in north London.

It was the Nineties. I was a librarian then and she was a reader, passing her books over the counter for me to discharge and stack on a trolley. As I did so, she flicked through the contents of another trolley, that week's new purchases waiting to be stamped and issued, and quietly talked about the books she'd just read. It was always other people's books, never her own. She lived close by with one of her daughters and was our most famous regular but also the most inconspicuous, usually in comfortable shoes and an old grey mac, always without a handbag, just a string bag for her books.

Much of her childhood in the Twenties was spent further up the hill, in Hampstead Village at 34 Well Walk, in a rented Queen Anne house on a street favoured by writers. John Keats once lived at No. 46 and D. H. Lawrence at No. 32. She told me she learnt to read when she was 4 and remembered sheep grazing on Hampstead Heath. In 1941, after leaving Oxford with first-class honours in

Penelope Fitzgerald, *The Means of Escape* (2000)
4th Estate · Pb · 176pp · £8.99 · ISBN 9780007105014

English Literature, she was working as a script editor at the BBC when mutual friends introduced her to Desmond Fitzgerald. They fell in love and got married but, all too soon, Desmond had to go away to fight in North Africa.

He returned with a Military Cross for gallantry but, over the ensuing years, it gradually became clear that he was an alcoholic. My father served in the same war and suffered from the same addiction, so I find it easy to imagine the tensions this caused within her family, the constant stress over money and the lack of stability.

Penelope became the main breadwinner, teaching at various institutions while writing reviews and essays for newspapers and magazines, including *Punch* and the *Times Literary Supplement*. She also wrote a biography of one of the Pre-Raphaelite artists, Edward Burne-Jones. However, her first fictional venture may well have been 'The Axe', a short story in the form of an office work report that gradually becomes increasingly gruesome. It was published in *The Times Anthology of Ghost Stories* in 1975 and is now in *The Means of Escape*. It's possible, as she once hinted, that she began writing fiction to amuse her husband. She certainly read to him during his last illness when he was in hospital. He died in 1976.

The Means of Escape contains nine additional stories and an excellent introduction by A. S. Byatt, who also knew her a little. In the Sixties they both taught at Westminster Tutors, a posh crammer which prepared would-be students for their Oxford or Cambridge entrance exams, and between tutorials they sometimes enjoyed a coffee together. Byatt found that Penelope 'appeared mild and retiring, [but she] could be suddenly sharp and incisive'. An observation that reminded me of an occasion when Penelope had taken part in a literary festival that I set up for Haringey Libraries.

At Wood Green library she sat with the audience, listening to the other authors read their work before it was her turn to do so. I sat next to her, feeling privileged and excited. Penelope was definitely the star that night. Not only had she won a Booker Prize for her third novel, *Offshore*, but she was about to read us a chapter from her most recent novel, *The Blue Flower*, the first novel by a non-American to win the National Book Critics Circle Award.

The hall was packed and I could tell that the audience was really looking forward to it, but first we had to listen to a lesser-known writer, a poet who, unfortunately, had no idea how clunky his poems were or how bored and restless his audience was growing. When at last he concluded and the audience rewarded him with a polite sprinkle of applause, he smiled and stepped forward. 'Shall I read you some more?' he asked. There was a shocked pause, an embarrassed silence, then Penelope intervened.

'Oh no, dear. That's quite enough.'

Her response seemed almost involuntary. She spoke in her normal speaking voice, not loudly, but into a silence that quickly turned into noisy clapping as the poet left the stage. I introduced her and then she gave her reading. As you might imagine, it went down extremely well. She wasn't so retiring when she read, quite the opposite, her confidently delivered words capturing everyone's attention. After the event, I offered to order her a taxi.

'I never take taxis,' she said. 'Prefer a bus. *Much* nicer.'

She must have been 80 by then. I watched her walk off down Wood Green High Street, alone and looking rather vulnerable on a dark evening, and hoped she'd get home safely. As usual, she wore her old grey mac and carried no handbag, only a white plastic bag containing her copy of her novel. I imagined her sitting on the double-decker, squeezed in with the other passengers, and wondered if she'd be listening to their conversations, noting how they looked. A writer, I thought – of course she prefers a bus.

She didn't just rely on observation. She was a scrupulous fact-checker, often coming into the library to browse through the Reference volumes that no one else seemed to touch. Reading *The Means of Escape*, I wondered if as well as researching distant times she might also have liked long-distance travel. Two of her stories are set in the southern hemisphere – one in Tasmania, one in New Zealand. Her characters include an elderly Turkish aunt giving a soirée, a malevolent Greek doctor and his intelligent assistant, and a group of young British artists painting *en plein air*, in Brittany.

In the story 'Beehernz', the deputy artistic director of the Midland Music Festival wants to ask a once-renowned pianist to give another performance. Nearly forty years earlier Beehernz, the pianist, had quietly announced his retirement because he'd found Mahler's Eighth Symphony *'too noisy'*. Now he lives on Reilig, a tiny island off the west coast of Scotland. Undeterred, the director optimistically draws up a contract and travels by ferry from Oban to Mull, from Mull to Iona, finally by small boat to Reilig. He arrives with two assistants only to find the pianist, now a frail old man in gumboots, living alone in a single-storey cottage with no radio, no books, no scores and a piano that makes no sound. He had no need of an audience 'in a kingdom of potatoes and seabirds'.

In her introduction, Byatt talks about Fitzgerald's exactness of language which is apparent in all her work and especially in the short stories. On first reading them I made the mistake of galloping through, rejoicing in the elegance of each sentence but not fully understanding the characters' dilemmas or decisions. It was only when I read them again, slowly, that so much more unfolded. In short stories, of course, it is often what is left out that says the most.

In her essay 'Following the Plot' (published in *House of Air*, 2005) Fitzgerald says: 'The short stories I wrote at the age of 8 or 9 did not bring me the success I hoped for, and years of formal education in English literature gradually taught me the uneasy moral status of plots. If they were of the extravagantly ingenious kind, they had to be "forgiven" or "over-looked" on behalf of the writer.'

The plots in her short stories are ingenious but extravagance is usually reserved for the imagery that cloaks them. The title story, 'The Means of Escape', set in Hobart in the 1850s, concerns a convict who first appears in church in front of the rector's daughter Alice:

'the head was hidden in some kind of sack like a butchered animal, or, since it had no eye holes, more like a man about to be hanged'.

He tells her he has escaped from the Model Penitentiary and plans to stow away on a ship about to depart for Portsmouth. He wants some women's clothing for a disguise. First Alice and then her friend Aggie agree to help him, but he disappears without their assistance. The mystery of how he disappears and who else helps him is only made clear to Alice eight months later when a letter arrives from Portsmouth. The reader is told that the letter, like so many other records of convict days, is now kept in the National Library of Tasmania. Of course this may also be a fiction, but it's easy to imagine Penelope coming across a real letter and conjuring up the story.

Her precisely chosen words allow time to flow across continents and through the centuries, evoking the smell of disappointment in a post-war London office, the look of a National Trust building with its herb and lavender garden, possibly suggested by Gertrude Jekyll, or the precious feel of a gilt medal given to an 11-year-old boy as a keepsake. Engraved on the medal is the date of his birthday – September 12, 1663.

In an old album I have another keepsake, a photograph taken by a Highgate colleague who, on learning that we were threatened with closure, persuaded everyone in the library to pose on the front steps. There we all are, the caretaker, myself, a library assistant and various members of the public. Our regulars. Standing at the foot of the steps and to one side, wearing her old grey mac and being carefully inconspicuous, as usual, is Penelope. In fact, although nobody gave it away, all of us knew by then just how famous she really was – a wonderful novelist, biographer and essayist. It wasn't until a little later when her collection was published, posthumously, that I realized she was also a remarkable short-story writer.

LINDA LEATHERBARROW's prize-winning and broadcast short stories are published in *Essential Kit* and *Funny Things, Families*.

'Tis Better to Have Loved and Lost?

CHRISTOPHER RUSH

Tennyson's *In Memoriam* (1850) is a poem about love and death, the two things which change all things – which is a powerful reason for reading what happens to be a powerful piece of writing, one of the key works of the nineteenth century, and one which has been described antithetically as the epitome of Victorian scepticism and of Christian faith. And there you have it: a great work of art precisely because it contains no single clear moral, despite its many pronouncements, but teaches us instead that life is a complex business which can't be diluted to the simplicity of a didactic dictum. The poem partakes rather of that suspension of decision which is the exact opposite of what we expect and get from propaganda, an art form best left to the politicians. Great writers never attempt to reduce human existence to a formula; there are no rights and wrongs, no clear-cut messages in any work of art, and that is why *In Memoriam* is an artistic triumph.

Another reason for reading the poem is that it isn't actually a poem, it's 132 poems, composed over seventeen years, which the author eventually arranged into an invented chronological order, with Christmases and anniversaries and flashbacks, before presenting it for publication as a single composition which it both is and isn't. So there are two ways to read it: either as it is presented, with its progress from grief and despair to recovery and hope of new life; or

Alfred, Lord Tennyson's *In Memoriam A. H. H.* (1850) is included in the Penguin edition of his *Selected Poems* (ed. Christopher Ricks): Pb · 432pp · £9.99 · ISBN 9780140424430.

recognizing that this was a superficial pattern imposed by the poet on poems that had been composed over a long period according to the mood of the moment, often expressing violent conflicts and clashes of ideas and emotions, and that had then been reshuffled to form a more coherent entity.

What is *In Memoriam* specifically about? It was begun in 1833 when Arthur Henry Hallam, Tennyson's close friend and fellow student at Trinity College, Cambridge, died suddenly while in Vienna of a cerebral haemorrhage. He was 22 and engaged to Tennyson's sister, Emily. Tennyson was grief-stricken and began to question the conventional Christian beliefs which were already under attack from other quarters.

Alfred, Lord Tennyson, attrib.
James Spedding, pencil, *c.* 1831
(© NPG)

So the poem is essentially an elegy: it opens a gate we all go through. We love, we fall in love, we lose our loved ones. Few of us would wish to die and be forgotten; fewer still would wish to forget those lost loved ones. The funeral service acts as a two-way outlet for this huge human emotion, followed in most cases either by a headstone or a scattering of ashes. After which comes, if we are lucky, the penned elegy, which can be as much about the bereaved as the departed, or even more so.

In Tennyson's case AHH was both a bosom companion and engaged to Emily, so his death was not only a personal tragedy but also a family one: the circumstances were ripe for a potentially profound and historic piece of writing, always assuming Tennyson could hold it together and balance his intellect and his emotions. He rose to the challenge.

> Old Yew, which graspest at the stones,
> That name the under-lying dead,

Thy fibres net the dreamless head,
Thy roots are wrapt about the bones.

The seasons bring the flower again
    And bring the firstling to the flock;
    And in the dusk of thee the clock
Beats out the little lives of men.

O not for thee the glow, the bloom,
    Who changest not in any gale,
    Nor branding summer suns avail
To touch thy thousand years of gloom:

And gazing on thee, sullen tree,
    Sick for thy stubborn hardihood,
    I seem to fail from out my blood
And grow incorporate into thee.

In Memoriam, No. 2

The evergreen yew is traditionally planted in graveyards as a symbol of eternal life, and as such is a familiar image in elegies. For Tennyson the yew represents the freedom he longs for: an escape and release from the seemingly endless and pointless cycle of birth and death, the change and decay of which there will be a lot more to follow in the sequence. Here the chosen images and epithets – dusk, gloom, sullen, stubborn – are hardly joyful ones but at least they offer an unchanging certainty, preferable to the fugitive hands of the clock that beats out our little lives. Better the tree's thousand years of gloom than the flashy futile kaleidoscope of human life.

So, there is envy as well as identification. Like many poets before and after him, like Keats envying the urn or nightingale, he yearns to be one with the world of the yew tree. And there is another important aspect of his envious longing. The tree enjoys a close contact with the lost loved one, a closeness which the bereaved poet has lost. It clutches at the headstone, head and bones; the actions of the roots and fibres suggest a human desire, the poet's desire to grasp his dead friend. Essentially the tree experiences an embrace which he longs to share, to be wrapped around Hallam's body.

And one more thing: as he stares at the envied yew, his yearning to embrace the dead appears to be fulfilled as he leaves his body and grows 'incorporate into thee'. There is a pun here on 'corpse', and also a double meaning in 'thee'. He has incorporated himself not only into the tree but by implication and extension into the body of his friend; he has entered him, in spirit at least. This is as close to necrophilia as a Victorian poet can come.

After that moment of grasped calm, Tennyson's emotions start to unravel. Sorrow becomes a cruel friend and a bitter priestess, offering false, mocking oracles which he struggles to reject. 'The stars', she whispers, 'blindly run.' When asleep he is at sea without a rudder, under a cloud of vague objectless anxieties, all somehow much better in the morning, as we all know: what seems insurmountable at 3 a.m. is not so bad at 8 a.m. But what happens when you can't sleep and get up to wander the streets? It is in this black mood that he approaches his dead friend's old home in poem No. 7:

> Dark house, by which once more I stand
>   Here in the long unlovely street,
>   Doors where my heart was used to beat
> So quickly, waiting for a hand,
>
> A hand that can be clasp'd no more –
>   Behold me, for I cannot sleep,
>   And like a guilty thing I creep
> At earliest morning to the door.
>
> He is not here; but far away
>   The noise of life begins again,
>   And ghastly through the drizzling rain
> On the bald street breaks the blank day.

This is the bleakest of the lyrics in which Tennyson describes himself haunting Hallam's house in the early hours 'like a guilty thing', which is an allusion to the opening scene of *Hamlet*, except that here, by a striking reversal, it is not the dead man but the mourner who appears as the guilty ghost and fulfils that role, a restless revenant, troubling the once happy home. Readers may regard the situation as fanciful and even contrived, but I confess to doing exactly the same thing after my first wife died young and I found myself out in the small hours saying her name to the stray dogs of dawn, haunting the street where we first set up house after we were married; and the 'long unlovely street' perfectly reflects the desolation I felt. Tennyson is open about his desire for tactile union; the image of the hand is used forty times in the sequence to express the loss of Hallam's presence and the poet's physical loneliness and longing for contact.

All to no avail: 'He is not here.' It's an even more striking allusion, the four flat stark monosyllables echoing the exact words of the angel to Mary Magdalene and the other Mary who came to the tomb of Jesus to anoint the body. They were weeping bitterly, and yet the four words which appear to offer no hope indicate in fact the wildest hope of all: the hope of resurrection. And suddenly Hallam is associated with the risen Christ and Tennyson becomes a weeping woman, a bride of Christ, the first of several instances in the sequence where the poet, in exploring his relationship with the dead Hallam, assumes the role of the female, as bride, widower and even mother. This has led some critics to suggest that his love for Hallam was the love that dare not speak its name – though I think it more likely that when a man loses a close friend and spends the next seventeen years of his life attempting to re-establish that contact with him, the friend is liable to assume the form of a lost love, which has more to do with the poetic process than with any sexual or romantic reality.

The reality now is that the new day brings no hope, no joy, only more of the same: 'The noise of life begins again', not the 'sound' or 'sounds' of life, because life without Hallam is a cacophonous monotony, without meaning or music.

Eliot called Tennyson the saddest of all the English poets, Auden called him the stupidest, adding that there was little about melancholia that he didn't know, and there was little else that he did know; and Shaw chipped in with his picture of a morbid and unhappy mystic, afraid of death, sex and God, and with the brains of a third-rate policeman. These are gibes as stupid as they are unjust; he was a master craftsman and a marathon man, revising and polishing his work to an extent that even Browning considered insane. But he was a professional. Unfortunately, he suffered from a number of disadvantages: he wasn't born poor, didn't die poor, was not misunderstood like Keats or drowned like Shelley, didn't suffer an early death, didn't reject the poet laureateship, was an idol of Queen Victoria, whom he met twice, and who told him what a comfort *In Memoriam* had been to her after the death of Albert – and oh yes, he also wrote 'The Charge of the Light Brigade'. An easy target then for critics.

In Memoriam is actually Tennyson's poetic journal, the private diary of a man confessing himself in public, and its compulsive hold on me has little to do with its strict chronological structure, rather its concentrated and sustained, yet loose, diurnal drive, the human moods swinging wildly, as they do, giving the poem its truthfulness and honesty.

Eliot felt that its faith was a poor paltry thing: if I do not believe I shall despair, therefore I must believe – and that it was the doubt that made it so real and so convincing. Tennyson's own view was that 'it's too hopeful, this poem, more than I am myself', while others felt that his personal faith was stronger than it appears in the poem; and others again, notably Charles Kingsley, championed the work as 'the noblest Christian poem which England has produced for two centuries', placing Tennyson on a pedestal with Milton.

Never trust the teller, trust the tale. And never trust the critic either, especially if he is one like the Reverend Kingsley, with an axe to grind. Tennyson had an axe to grind too. He had known Miss Emily Sellwood since childhood and had proposed to her (twice) unsuccessfully – she considered his religious beliefs did not conform sufficiently to her own. The first engagement was suspended and altogether it took him a decade and a half to get her to the altar. It's no coincidence that the marriage eventually took place just a few weeks after the publication of *In Memoriam*. One critic called the poem his letter of seduction to her, a proof of his Christianity. A stupid poet? Tennyson knew what he was doing, and doubtless also knew the old saying that when Judas Iscariot goes out, he meets Judas Iscariot. Different readers found and still find in the poem precisely what they want to find, which was probably exactly as Tennyson intended.

Ultimately what matters is not the poet or his critics but the poem itself. It is fiercely fearless and rich in the paradoxical possibilities that lie at the heart of the human situation, stating in this case that it is better to have loved and lost than never to have loved at all, while other parts of it whisper to hurt hearts that perhaps it's not, perhaps it's better to have lived less and suffered less pain. I kept a copy of the poem in my pocket when I took a donkey across the Cévennes after the death of my first wife in 1993; and when later I decided to write a book charting my journey from grief to recovery, it was Tennyson who was my model, my Virgil and Dante, my guide through hell. His poem is a love letter not principally to Emily Sellwood but to Arthur Hallam, and I have never read a more sustained, searching, devastating and bitter-sweet letter to the dead. It is a masterpiece.

CHRISTOPHER RUSH has been writing for thirty-five years. His books include the memoirs *To Travel Hopefully* and *Hellfire and Herring*, and *Will*, a novel about Shakespeare. His latest novel, *Penelope's Web*, was published in 2015.

The Sound of Chariots

SUE GAISFORD

The light was fading fast and the museum would soon close. A crepuscular hush was stealthily invading the Roman galleries when, shockingly, came the unmistakable loud, tinkling sound of hard cash, of many coins falling from a great height. Surely there wasn't a fruit machine in the ancient fortress of Colchester? Of course not. At the end of the room a large screen showed a vast, applauding amphitheatre, and a Roman chariot, with a shower of denarii cascading into it. A lad, strolling towards us, looked nonchalant. He had won, fair and square, loud and clear.

It was a brilliant video game. You just had to pick up and twitch the leather reins and the race was on. And it was clearly dead easy. But actually it wasn't. I'm a good driver but those four unbiddable beasts took off like a Maserati: in my careful hands they crashed into the wall and careered into the path of other chariots, rightly earning me the derision of the whole assembled (virtual) throng and resulting, twice, in disqualification. Luckily, the museum staff signalled that it was time to leave before further humiliation.

Rosemary Sutcliff knew about chariots. In the first of her four Roman books, *The Eagle of the Ninth* (1954), her young hero, the centurion Marcus Flavius Aquila, politely suggests to his British friend Cradoc that the British are all charioteers. Cradoc replies (accurately): 'The British can all drive after a fashion; not every one is a charioteer.' Marcus, however, is the real thing, the best in his Legion. Elegantly he slaloms Cradoc's four strong little black stallions through planted spears, and then, reaching open land, he gives them their heads and they are off, at full gallop:

To Marcus, that moment was always like being born from one kind of life into another. So must an arrow feel when it leaves the bow! It had been hot and sultry in the old life, but in this one the cool wind flowed against him like water, pressing his thin scarlet tunic into his body, singing past his ears above the soft thunder of the ponies' flying hooves. He crouched lower, feeling the chariot floor buoyant and vibrating under his wide-set feet, feeling the reins quick with life in his hands, his will flowing out along them to the flying team, and their response flowing back to him, so that they were one.

'On, brave hearts! On, bold and beautiful!'

. . . The forest verge spun by, the fern streaked away beneath flying hooves and whirring wheels. He and his team were a comet shooting down the bright ways of the sky; a falcon stooping against the sun.

I read this chapter last week to a group of residents in a care home. A captive audience, mostly they come along just for a change of armchair; often they snooze, as if half-listening to a bedtime story. On Thursday however – for the first time in years – they all stayed wide awake, and at the end they all but applauded with sheer exhilaration.

If you ever wondered how Rosemary Sutcliff achieved such widespread, lasting and affectionate fame, this passage gives you one answer. Her imagination was unbounded by time, space or experience, and she could write better than any other children's writer of her time.

She was a tiny woman, seriously disabled by Still's disease before she was three. Still's is a rare auto-immune disease, a kind of wandering arthritis, which attacks various joints, apparently at random, causing excruciating pain. If contracted after adolescence, it can disappear – in my own case for years – returning only occasionally; the damage, thank goodness, is seldom permanent. It is a different matter if

caught in childhood. The damaged joints remain distorted, and the effect is crippling. Rosemary was two and a half when it began, and it lasted, in active form, until she was five. At first, arsenic in her medication caused terrifying hallucinations of wolves gathering in the shadowy corners of her room, and a black panther under her bed. Later she endured many operations and spells in hospital, eventually learning to walk again, though never easily. She came late to reading, and she left school early to become a painter of miniatures – larger canvases being deemed too unwieldy. But, as she remarks in her luminous memoir, *Blue Remembered Hills*, painting miniatures had cramped her style, and she took instead to writing: 'One can write as big as one needs; no canvas is too large to be unmanageable.'

The battle scenes in the first two of her Roman books superbly demonstrate that narrative command. Sutcliff liked Westerns, and they come to mind in *The Eagle of the Ninth* when the Romans are attempting to defend their fort from attack by the rebellious native Britons: desperately, they summon reinforcements – whose arrival, very nearly too late, is ultimately heralded by a type of smoke-signal. Yet the scene is more dramatic than anything dreamed up in Hollywood: the British thunder towards the fray, curved and deadly knives whirling on their chariot wheels, and Marcus leads a Roman testudo out towards them in determined, disciplined formation ('more a gigantic woodlouse than a tortoise', Rosemary observes) before commanding it to disperse and courting certain death in a brilliant, gallant leap upon the driver of the leading war-chariot, a man once his friend, now become his deadly enemy.

Similarly, near the end of *The Silver Branch* (1957) comes a nail-biting, heart-pounding account of the epic battle, nearly a hundred years later, that famously ended in the destruction of Calleva (modern Silchester, where still the evidence of former glories and catastrophes can be glimpsed). As the battering-ram beats down the great gates of the basilica, and the horde of screaming barbarians pour through, with slaughter in their hearts, fire leaps up to the rafters, engulfing those sheltering there in waves of black, acrid smoke. High up in the blazing building the young surgeon Justin Aquila is, like his ancestor Marcus, careless of his own life – ignoring the advancing flames he cradles an elderly, fatally wounded gladiator and comforts him by conjuring up memories of the crowds who cheered his victories long ago, in the arenas of Rome. It is magnificent stuff.

At the same time, the attention to detail is phenomenal. Once, as a child, Rosemary was punished for refusing to eat her aunt's pudding – which she declared both looked and tasted pale grey. They sat her on the grass at the edge of the Downs and left her there, confident that she could not move to run away. Not remotely chastened, she began minutely examining the foot or two of turf around her, discovering a tiny forest of thyme, scarlet pimpernel, clover, cinquefoil and eyebright, wherein lived snails, ladybirds, beetles. 'Thank you, Aunt Lucy,' she later wrote, 'for your pale grey pudding.'

From such close observation of nature comes her gift for description. She loves describing light, for example. Candle flames are often the shape of a crocus, but the glow coming through thick Roman glass, or illuminating a face in the shadows, or beginning to disperse the darkness of night is never just yellow but the colour of a primrose or daffodil, a buttercup or marigold – or sometimes runny honey. And when Marcus, slowly recovering after that desperate leap at a British war-chariot, lies on a stone bench in his uncle's garden, gazing up into the 'blown, blue heights of heaven', he hears birds, down in the forest, singing with 'that note of clear-washed surprise that belongs to early spring'.

The centuries during which the Romans occupied Britain can seem impossibly far away. Yet the human urge to imagine what life was like here, so long ago, cannot easily be suppressed. In our part of Sussex, there is a scrubby piece of Wealden woodland sloping down to a little, once navigable river. The Romans built a road there, from some small iron-workings on the hill. Nobody goes there now and it is very overgrown, but scratch around and you can find carefully shaped and regularly placed kerbstones, and, if you really try, you can hear and see those legions marching down the hill in strict and disciplined formation . . .

Kipling saw them, and put them into *Puck of Pook's Hill*, and Rosemary's uncle read Kipling to her long before she could read herself. And she took him further. Her Romans are as real as your neighbours, as heroic or weak, as appealing or appalling. She describes their ambitions, their families and, most of all, their adventures. The first of them, Marcus, though now lame, resolves to discover the fate of the lost Ninth Legion, which had been commanded by his father. Following the Saturnalia Games (another splendid set piece) he buys a slave, only to release him into freedom, and the two of them travel through the wild north, even beyond Hadrian's Wall, into a land of dangerous, pagan tribesmen, to discover the truth. In the course of their adventures, they retrieve the legion's eagle, now sadly wingless, along with a great emerald signet ring, bearing an intaglio dolphin, which Marcus's father had once owned.

In *The Silver Branch,* Justin, his descendant, arrives in Britain from Beersheba and encounters Flavius, a soldier who now wears that ring and proves to be his cousin. They too travel north to the Wall, though the political landscape has now changed and the Empire is beginning to fracture. Ultimately, they assemble their own ramshackle band of brothers into a legion of sorts, aiming to topple Allectus the

Traitor. There are echoes of the Second World War here, as they plot
to send refugees from the south coast over to France, by dead
of night. Their activities are discovered, and Paulinus, the mild-
mannered and generous facilitator of these escapes, helps them get
away, at the cost of his own life. One of their gang is a young
centurion, no longer able to countenance the cruelty of Allectus. On
hearing of the sacrifice of Paulinus, he murmurs a few words: 'Greater
love hath no man . . .' Justin thinks it sounds as though he were
quoting someone else. Later, he draws a fish in the sand, and Justin
remembers his own time in Judea when he saw that sign, 'something
to do with a man called the Christos . . . who had been executed
more than two hundred years ago, but it seemed that he still had
followers'.

How cleverly she manipulates her readers. We are suddenly reminded that these people, so real and immediate to us now, are the
fictional inhabitants of a world long since almost buried and lost. At
the same time, she gives them, too, a folk memory. On another
occasion, the two cousins discuss their common ancestor, Marcus. As
happens in families, his great heroic story has been watered down
until, as Flavius puts it, 'he was lamed in some tribal uprising or
other', while his tremendous journey in search of the eponymous
eagle becomes 'some sort of an adventure in the North, in his wild
young days'. We, of course, know better.

This is the best kind of historical fiction, far too good to be
limited to children's bookshelves. Rosemary Sutcliff's characters
are immediately believable, and she conjures the lives they lead using
every sense. We know what Roman Britain looked, tasted, felt,

Charles Keeping

sounded and smelt like and we can even prove some of her apparently wild assertions. When Justin and Flavius manage to hide in a hypocaust, a brief visit to, say, the site at Binchester, shows just how possible that would have been. Their adventures are set among real historical buildings and events, often provoked by real figures of history. Even the wingless eagle exists still, in Reading Museum, having been discovered in the remains of the burnt-out basilica of Calleva. It is immensely pleasing to have such a plausible – albeit complicated and circuitous – explanation of how it got there.

SUE GAISFORD's journalism has appeared in *The Economist*, *Country Living* and virtually everything in between. She enjoys interviewing very old people and visiting ancient monuments.

Slightly Foxed will be reissuing all four of Rosemary Sutcliff's Roman Britain novels – *The Eagle of the Ninth*, *The Silver Branch*, *Frontier Wolf* and *The Lantern Bearers* – as a set in a limited and numbered cloth-bound edition of 2,000 copies.

The Eagle of the Ninth (248pp) and *The Silver Branch* (216pp) are available now. *Frontier Wolf* and *The Lantern Bearers* will be published in September 2020 and can be ordered in advance (subscribers per copy for all titles: UK & Eire £17, Overseas £19; non-subscribers: UK & Eire £19, Overseas £21). All prices include post and packing. Copies may be ordered by post (53 Hoxton Square, London N1 6PB), by phone (020 7033 0258) or via our website www.foxedquarterly.com.

Porridge and the Shorter Catechism

MORAG MCINNES

Food is an expression of a culture, a reminder of your roots. I inherited a battered copy of *Glasgow Cookery*, peppered with my granny's authoritative biro. It transports me to a simpler time. Liver and bacon every Wednesday, cod in lumpy sauce on Fridays. She scalded and plucked chickens. I'll never forget the smell of the feathers. She was what's called a good plain cook – lots of pancakes, jammy scones and barley thickened soups. But it would never have occurred to her that the way she cooked – using every last bit of an animal, turning hard bread into puddings – was interesting in itself, or that it could teach anyone about what it meant to be Scottish. For that insight we are indebted to a remarkable Orcadian woman.

Florence Marian McNeill, known as Floss, understood the importance of regional dishes. You may know her better as a folklorist; but without *The Scots Kitchen*, first published in 1929, she'd never have begun collecting the scraps of song, story, local traditions and unlikely remedies which grew over the years to become her definitive work on folklore, *The Silver Bough*. She was born in Holm, in Orkney, in 1885, the eighth of twelve children of the Manse. Her father, Daniel, was not a typical Free Kirk character – he sang, played fiddle, liked a dram and a dance. His wife Jessie was austere, self-effacing. She had wanted to be a doctor or a missionary, but such options weren't open to her. Instead, she inspired her bairns.

In summer the old Manse overflowed with young life . . . one

Florence Marian McNeill, *The Scots Kitchen: Its Traditions and Recipes* (1929)
Birlinn · Pb · 368pp · £14.99 · ISBN 9781780273013

never knew what the winds would blow in – an Oxford don or a packman . . . the sea before our window was blue and green and purple, and brown sailed fishing vessels passed up and down the sound. Owld Jock would climb the long loan from the village with his creel of silver herring, and Beenie, who presided in the kitchen, would run down to the gate for an ashetful, and serve them up for supper all frizzling in their golden coats of oatmeal.

You don't have to be a sociologist to see how she has neatly pin-pointed what modern chefs, with their proud cries of 'locally sourced', can never return to – a world where you could see the link between the fishing boats outside your window and the 'frizzling' (what a perfect word) herring. No big supermarkets or air miles – just the local van, 'a miniature shop on wheels . . . he never failed to reach down a big glass jar, and, with a "Ha'e, bairns", fill our small outstretched hands with gaily coloured fruit drops that sparkled in the sun'.

It wasn't, of course, all wonderful. 'Soon we were in the chill embrace of the northern winter . . . breakfast and tea were served in lamplight, and in the long dark evenings fearful shadows lurked . . . shut off from the outer world by raging winds and seas, we lived largely in a world of fancy, inspired by song and story.'

Floss matriculated from Glasgow in 1912, a contemporary of James Bridie the playwright and the left-wing politician Jimmy Maxton. Her novel *The Road Home* describes some of the routine sexism she encountered. Women had to watch from the galleries during the debates which the university held regularly. They weren't allowed to stand on the rostrum and take part. 'It's a man's show . . . exactly alike in their black and white uniforms, like rows of penguins . . .'

The novel also charts a painful love affair. However close the account is to the truth, she never married, and devoted the rest of her life to Scottishness, liberal causes and the folk customs she'd first heard about from Beenie. Perhaps

her only indulgence was her love of good food and drink; it connected her to that happier past, when, like her fictional heroine Morag, she was 'a shocking little gourmet. She could tell you just the specialities of each farm and cottage where she went to tea, and could warn you against those good wives whose scones were stodgy, whose butter tasted of turnips, or who let their tea infuse too long.'

The Scots Kitchen seems almost inevitable. Floss's mother was from the east of Scotland, her father from the west, and she was a northerner who loved the Border ballads. It was a perfect triangle of rural experience. Scotland was on the brink of a political and literary renaissance. A book which was part social history and memoir, part recipes, which put her country's food and customs down for all to enjoy, and also allowed her to express her ebullient, trenchant personality, hit all the right notes.

The moment you read the preface you know you're travelling with a feisty companion. 'In Scotland today, there is of good home cooking less and less . . . neither the variety nor the respect for quality.' This in 1929 – imagine if you took her to a burger bar!

Glance at the appendices, and you're hooked. Grosset means gooseberry, from the French. It yields two quotes: 'A randy-like woman with a basket of grossets' (that's John Galt), and 'They will jump at them in Edinburgh like a cock at a grosset.' That's from a Scott novel – she loves Sir Walter.

'The proverbial Scot has been reared on porridge and the Shorter Catechism,' she tells us, 'a rigorous diet but highly beneficial to those possessed of sound digestive organs.' Her footnotes are a source of great joy. Carlyle said Macaulay was an honest, good sort of fellow made out of oatmeal and she thinks he might have returned the compliment. Girls keep a muslin bag of oatmeal in their ewer overnight to improve their complexions. Teething babies get an oatcake with a ring in it to bite on. The Bonnach Solain (the Gaelic term for a bannock, or scone) was highly salted, to induce dreams which foretold the future.

The mix of erudition and the unexpected is delightful. Add in her love of songs, poems, names – Veal Flory, Wind Blown Fish, Whim Wham, Clapshot, Inky Pinky, plus her magpie-like collection of gems from other writers – and it becomes a paean to Scottishness.

There are using cookbooks and having ones. You can use *The Scots Kitchen*. You can prepare haggis ('make incisions in the heart and liver to allow the blood to flow out . . . leave the windpipe hanging out over the pot to let out any impurities') but if you are faint-hearted with regard to cleaning out 'the great bag' and cutting away 'skins, black parts and superfluities of gristle', perhaps it's best to make for the footnote. 'It is a thoroughly democratic dish,' we learn, 'equally available and equally honoured in castle and croft. The use of the paunch of the animal as the receptacle for the ingredients gives that touch of barbarism so dear to the Scots people.' She bats away the suggestion that haggis might be 'one of the nobler legacies of France' (they allude to it as *le pain bénit d'Ecosse*) and reminds those who might sneer at its simplicity that 'that most aesthetic of nations, the ancient Greeks, had a haggis of their own, immortalised by Aristophanes'.

There you have Floss in full flow; clever, funny, partial, patriotic.

The rest of her life was less kind. *The Silver Bough*, her seminal work, was twenty years in the making. She died in Edinburgh, 'in sadly constrained and lonely circumstances', aged 88. In this early book she's in her prime.

MORAG MACINNES is an Orcadian writer. She has never tried to make her own haggis but her scones are passable. The illustrations in this article are by Iain McIntosh.

Challenging the Old Gang

MICHAEL BARBER

As a beneficiary of the Welfare State and the Permissive Society – to name just two of their life-enhancing achievements – I owe an enormous debt to the liberal intelligentsia who, in the teeth of opposition from the Old Gang, brought them to pass. But who were these irreverent shock troops and what motivated them? The answer is given by one of their standard bearers, Noel Annan (1916–2000), in his dazzling group portrait *Our Age* (1990), which is not only a joy to read but also a wonderful crib for anyone studying the social history of Britain from the 1920s to the 1960s.

Lord Annan was that rare phenomenon, a public figure who could write, the greatest prose stylist of his generation in the opinion of some. During the war, from which he emerged in the rank of Lieutenant-Colonel, with an OBE and a head full of secrets, he was posted to the Joint Intelligence Staff, preparing the daily briefings for the chiefs of staff and the prime minister. This highly pressurized assignment involved swiftly interpreting masses of information and then expressing it succinctly and cogently, a skill on display in this book, the scope of which left reviewers gasping. 'How could one man', asked Frank Kermode, 'know so much about so much?'

In addition to his mastery of detail Annan displays a wicked gift for observation. His appraisal of F. R. Leavis is exemplary: 'he cultivated to perfection the sneer which he used like an oyster knife, inserting it into the shell of his victim, exposing him with a quick

---

Noel Annan, *Our Age: Portrait of a Generation* (1990), is out of print, but we can obtain second-hand copies.

turn of the wrist, and finally flipping him over and inviting his audience to discard him as tainted and inedible'. He was also, as another reviewer noted, a master of the erudite aside, 'uttered *sotto voce*, as it were, as the port goes round'. Thus Guy Burgess 'had the look of a man who had just stepped off the Golden Arrow after a night in the Rue de Lappe'. But because he wrote most often for the *New York Review of Books*, Annan was beyond the reach of many British readers. *Our Age*, much of it derived from his journalism, makes good this lacuna.

The title of Annan's book invokes one of his mentors, the witty, charismatic Oxford don and self-styled leader of the Immoral Front, Sir Maurice Bowra, who used it to describe the two or three generations, almost all of them male, from which sprang the liberal insurgents referred to above.

Secular, pluralist, cosmopolitan and sexually flexible, valuing brains above birth or money, they rejected the 'insufferable ideal' of the English gentleman and its concomitant, the 'good form' inculcated at the public schools that most of them had attended. Bowra's loathing for this code began in 'the mud, shit and decomposing corpses' of the Western Front, which he experienced as a young gunnery officer. 'Whatever you hear about the war,' he told Cyril Connolly, 'remember it was far worse: inconceivably bloody – nobody who wasn't there can imagine what it was like.'

Convinced that the Old Gang's ironclad complacency had compounded the slaughter in Flanders, Bowra, says Annan, 'embodied the spirit of those who wanted to be done with the war and good form'. An unrepentant pagan, he thought a lot of what you fancy did you good. 'Pleasure, vitality and spontaneity were his delight; caginess, philistinism, pretentiousness and pomposity his prey.'

Introduced to Bowra by another of his mentors, the Cambridge don Dadie Rylands, Annan swiftly fell under his spell. Like Rylands, Bowra was homosexual, and I think it's fair to assume that this was also true of Annan as an undergraduate, not least because consenting adults at

King's, his Cambridge college, could do pretty much as they pleased, always provided they did not offend the porters or bedmakers.

By then, the late Thirties, an enormous gap had opened between intelligent young people like Annan and the fogeys set in authority over them. Homosexuality, to which Annan devotes two chapters, 'became a way of jolting respectable opinion and mocking the Establishment'. It was also, for the 'buttoned-up' alumni of boys' boarding schools, an uncomplicated arrangement. Unused to chatting up girls, who were equally gauche and understandably reluctant to 'go all the way', these chaps regarded heterosexual sex, said Annan, 'as a choice between bores and whores'.

Eventually they would reform the law on homosexuality, just as they would those on divorce, abortion and obscenity. But against these humane initiatives must be set the baleful legacy of the Cambridge spies. Their discovery, says Annan, 'turned into a long-running inquest upon the culture, morality and patriotism of intellectuals of Our Age that the coroner kept on adjourning as spy after spy fell out of the cupboard' (or should it be closet?). Annan does not attempt to exonerate the spies, two of whom, Blunt and Burgess, he knew. But he rejects the notion, peddled by hacks like Chapman Pincher, that Cambridge was to blame, pointing out that Bletchley Park, the most successful intelligence source of any nation during the war, was inviolate, despite its nucleus being recruited from the same slightly suspect university circles as the spies.

Well, yes. But I can't resist repeating an anecdote told me by the writer Simon Raven, who enjoyed a rackety four years at King's just after the war. Distressed by his follies, dons like Rylands and Annan (then Assistant Tutor) urged Raven to be '"more like Ant Blunt. He had a lot of fun like you, but he worked hard, he behaved nicely, and unlike you he was a good socialist. *Be more like Blunt*," they said. So when Blunt was exposed I sent them all postcards saying, "Thank God I wasn't more like Blunt." Wasn't answered by many of them, I can tell you!'

For non-doctrinaire liberals like Annan the late Thirties were a profoundly depressing time. The Left had got its knickers in a twist, arguing against rearmament lest they be 'tricked into another war', yet urging the government to intervene in Spain against Franco. Meanwhile it was clear that Chamberlain, and the upper classes who supported him, were willing to do a deal with Hitler on the grounds that my enemy's enemy is my friend.

In the event, 'Our Age' did very well out of the war, the social consequences of which, in particular the expansion of universities, worked to their advantage. Brains were given their due. It was no longer such a defect to be 'too clever by half'. Writing in 1963, by which time he had been elected Provost of King's, Annan insisted that 'intellect' was what universities existed for. Everything else was secondary. 'A university is dead if the dons cannot in some way communicate to the students the struggle to produce out of the chaos of human experience some grain of order won by the intellect.'

So, for a season, the liberal intelligentsia enjoyed a place in the sun. The governing class, whatever their politics, accepted the need for change. British society became less deferential and more free-wheeling, a transformation that accelerated in the Sixties, when 'sexual intercourse began' and to be young was very heaven. But if sexual relations flourished, industrial relations did not, with dire consequences for the economy. Here was one aspect of modern life against which the intelligentsia had set its face. Whatever their differences — and Annan is at pains to emphasize how irreconcilable were, say, F. R. Leavis and Bloomsbury — they were united in their contempt for industry and business. E. M. Forster, whom Annan describes as his guru, had exposed the contradictions of this ethos fifty years before in *Howards End*. The arty, intelligent and compassionate Schlegels might be nicer and worthier than the money-grubbing Wilcoxes, but as *rentiers* they live indirectly on the wealth produced by the Wilcoxes.

And when the money runs out? Annan, who in 1966 left King's

to become Provost of University College, London, a much more challenging role, saw the writing on the wall. The Good Life was unsustainable without a sound economic base. Cue Margaret Thatcher, the ruthless champion of entrepreneurial Conservatism who made a bonfire of subsidies and established the market as the sole judge of what was valuable in life. Though he must have winced at her apparent indifference to the arts, Annan, unlike many of his coevals, saw the point of Thatcher. The closed shop and other restrictive practices had to be abolished if the country was to pay its way. And, sadly, universities could no longer expect a blank cheque.

Annan accepts that 'every generation turns on its fathers', but he is unwilling to turn the other cheek. To the charge brought by Roger Scruton that 'Our Age' lacked 'experience of the sacred and the erotic, of mourning and of holy dread', he responds, 'Our Age thought they had done rather well by the erotic but were prepared to admit they were a bit short on holy dread.'

'Holy dread' was certainly no concern of Annan's great friend Sir Isaiah Berlin, who said he was 'tone-deaf to God'. Berlin was preoccupied with the human condition, and according to Annan he wrote 'the truest and the most moving of all interpretations of life that my own generation made'. Some of what he said was disconcerting, like his assertion that good ends conflict: you cannot exercise mercy without cheating justice, to take one example. He was a champion of 'negative liberty' – the right to be left alone – and rejected ideology as irrevocably as religion.

In the address he gave at Sir Isaiah's memorial service in January 1998 Annan, quoting from one of his obituaries, said 'the respectful silence that met his death . . . shows that intellectuals can still be prized as civilizing influences in Britain'. I very much doubt if that is still the case, but it might serve as an epitaph for 'Our Age'.

MICHAEL BARBER interviewed Lord Annan forty years ago for *The Roads to Munich*, a radio series he wrote and presented about Appeasement.

Hauntings

MICHÈLE ROBERTS

As a Catholic teenager fascinated by sex but forbidden to practise it, I read about it instead, nourishing my hectic imagination on anything from John Donne's poetry to *Lolita* to my father's copies of *Men Only*. Simultaneously I devoured memoirs by nuns, just in case my religious vocation won out.

Looking back, I see that I was trapped by psychological splits I could not articulate. The nuns at my old-fashioned convent school passed on the Church's message that the body was opposed to and inferior to the mind. Men, lined up with soul and mind, had higher status than women, in that they could become priests. Women, lined up with body, had a special, lower status as mothers, ideally full-time. Sexual pleasure outside marriage was wicked. I was a swot, therefore not truly feminine. I thought I was a freak. Better perhaps to rise above gender, enter the cloister and divert passion to God. So when in the local public library I came across Dorothy L. Sayers's 1935 detective novel *Gaudy Night*, it seemed to speak to me directly. Set in Shrewsbury, a fictional Oxford women's college based on Somerville, Sayers's alma mater, it features a young writer of detective fiction, Harriet Vane, struggling with contradictions around love and sex but finally able to resolve them. The book became my talisman.

Aged 14, I read *Gaudy Night* simply as a tantalizing romance masquerading as a thriller. Rereading it now I see it as a ghost story, its form demanded by its subject matter. The ghosts float across the text

Dorothy L. Sayers, *Gaudy Night* (1935)
Hodder · Pb · 576pp · £9.99 · ISBN 9781473621404

as metaphors that are not merely decorative, as elements of style, but fundamental to the plot, which has to do, crucially, with language, written and spoken: language stolen, repressed, destroyed.

The novel opens with Harriet being invited by Mary Stokes, a friend from undergraduate days, to accompany her to a Gaudy at Shrewsbury. After graduation, Sayers tells us, Mary 'had married and scarcely been heard of; except that she haunted the College with a sick persistence, never missing an Old Students meeting or a Gaudy'.

Somerville College, Oxford, 1934. Courtesy of the Principal and Fellows

If Mary has haunted the College, Harriet is haunted by it, trying to ignore 'the whimpering ghost of her dead youth'. Returning to Oxford, she feels 'a chill qualm . . . the iron hand of the past gripping one's entrails' because her old innocence – intellectual and moral – has been lost. She has had extra-marital sex and been punished for it. Had up for the murder of her lover Philip Boyes, she has been proved not guilty only thanks to the intervention of the aristocratic sleuth Lord Peter Wimsey.

As a writer of detective fiction, Harriet invents plots that are coldly mechanical. In this way she tries to repel the phantoms lurking in the corners of her mind: 'Philip Boyes was dead, and the nightmares that had haunted the ghastly midnight of his passing were gradually fading away.'

Wandering in the quad late at night, after the Gaudy dinner, Harriet sees something white 'fluttering . . . across the trim turf'. This 'ghost' is a sheet of paper with an ugly, sadistic drawing on it. A second sheet of paper bears a message seemingly meant for her: 'You dirty murderess. Aren't you ashamed to show your face?'

Soon afterwards, the dons ask Harriet to return to the college to investigate this cross between a poltergeist and a poison-pen writer. Anonymous letters are being sent and obscene messages scrawled on walls. Books by female scholars are defaced. The college library is vandalized, the volumes removed and flung about, and the walls adorned with inscriptions in letters a foot high, 'all of the most unseemly sort'. They are cleaned off by the college servants: whatever is being expressed must be denied.

These nuisances occur at night, the time when ghosts classically walk. Harriet comments to the Dean that perhaps the perpetrator is somebody with a mania for creating disturbance in order to enjoy the fun and the Dean agrees: 'like those tiresome children who throw furniture about and the servants who pretend to be ghosts'.

This reference to Henry James's *The Turn of the Screw* is just one of *Gaudy Night*'s literary allusions. Sayers's prose is stalked by the ghosts of other texts. Each chapter is introduced by a quotation from the work of writers such as John Donne, Richard Burton, Francis Bacon and Shakespeare. And when Harriet consults Peter Wimsey about the case they talk to each other in a non-stop flow of esoteric literary quotations.

Gaudy Night seems haunted by Sayers's anxieties. Writing at a time when the genre of detective fiction was seen as lowbrow, the highly educated Sayers seems ambivalent about how her novels are classified by critics. While determined to prove her literary credentials she also, via her caricatures of the poseurs Harriet meets at literary cocktail parties, mocks fashionable modernism. (Harriet's dead lover Philip Boyes, readers of *Strong Poison* will remember, was apparently a pretentious, sub-Lawrentian novelist: no wonder Sayers killed him off.) The undergraduates at Shrewsbury are fascinated by the talk Harriet delivers on her novels; she fantasizes that a School of Detective Fiction would produce 'a goodly crop of Firsts'.

The ghost theme dictates Harriet's choice of disguise. To conceal the real reason for her return to the college, she dons her scholar's persona and embarks on a study of Sheridan Le Fanu, the celebrated Victorian writer of ghost stories. By night she patrols the college corridors, wandering like a phantom. Her dreams are peopled by phantoms, her unacknowledged desire for Peter Wimsey among them. One evening, while she is writing in her room, in mid-paragraph comparing Le Fanu with Wilkie Collins and the latter's 'ghouls and ghaisties', the uncanny erupts: all the lights fuse and the poltergeist, a dark shape, races across the quad.

Harriet's interrupted paragraph on ghosts remains unfinished as she jumps up and gives chase. The ghosts in *Gaudy Night* jump up in much the same way. They perform as images of language not yet spoken, stories that need to be concluded. Harriet fails to piece the story together, ignoring the clues dropped by one of the college servants, despite realizing that she 'is . . . haunted by nervous terrors'. It is Peter Wimsey, less troubled than Harriet by personal conflicts around sex and work, who is able to use simple reasoning to get at the truth.

The malevolence that has been unleashed turns on a question of loyalty to one's sexual partner versus loyalty to the ideals of scholarship. A certain recent event seems to have triggered the outrages: the arrival of a new Fellow in college. From her Peter elicits details of some fraudulent work she encountered some years back, before taking up her new post at Shrewsbury, when examining an MA history thesis. Its author, she discovered, falsified his findings, and even stole and destroyed the texts that proved otherwise. Failed and disgraced, he finally killed himself or, as the furiously loyal poison-pen writer saw it, was driven to his death by words written on a worthless, 'dirty bit of paper'.

The return of the repressed accordingly sees the return of dirty bits of paper flung about Shrewsbury, texts whose obscene wording glosses unbearable sorrow and anger. The poison-pen writer's confession, when finally it comes, is a monologue allowing for no response; very unlike the swift, elegant wordplay Harriet and Peter enjoy.

The novel's cultural landscape resonated powerfully for me, reading in the 1960s. A commitment to writing seemed incompatible with a commitment to marriage and children. The Shrewsbury dons are all celibate: like nuns, they have made their choice of fulfilment. I identified with Harriet, who until the end of the novel remains torn between the calm life of the mind and the turbulent joys of the body. She ponders: 'could there ever be any alliance between the intellect and the flesh?'

Feminism offers her little help and remains a spectre prowling the novel's margins. It makes Harriet uncomfortable, since it appears linked to intolerance and humourlessness. Miss Hillyard, the History Tutor, who voices openly feminist opinions about injustice, is presented as harsh, bitter and sexually disappointed. Unable to admit her passionate attraction to Peter Wimsey, indeed mortified by it, Harriet takes herself late at night to the Fellows Garden, her sanctuary, the *hortus conclusus*, the enclosed garden symbolizing virginity in medieval poetry, and becomes a kind of ghost: 'the figure walking swiftly up and down, up and down . . . the rustle of its long skirt upon the grass'.

Once what everyone has agreed to call the College Ghost has been identified, challenged and heard out, Harriet is able to resolve her dilemmas. The ghost has been laid by having its tragic story told, and so now Harriet decides to write detective novels that will have more real life, more real feeling in them, even if writing in this way will 'hurt like hell'. She and Peter begin to imagine creating a new story together. They will rewrite the marriage plot. They will pursue a marriage of equals. Harriet will continue writing. It will help, of course, that marrying a wealthy man she will have servants and no money worries.

Another spectre haunting the plot is that of class and class divisions. The university is presented by Sayers as an ideal community, as is Shrewsbury College before the disturbances begin. However, the college is an institution structured by hierarchies of class and money that separate the highly educated dons from the less well-educated servants as though they are different species. The latter may wear smart uniforms and be kindly treated, but they are locked into their wing at night like 'caged animals', as the Bursar tartly observes. Various undergraduates are described as speaking with 'a common accent' or as 'having unrefined antecedents'. Are they and the scouts more likely to commit crimes than those educated in private schools?

Aged 14, snobbish and priggish as well as ardent and rebellious, I didn't see any of this. Dorothy Sayers's work simply offered a possible solution to my own mystery. Using a kind of reasoning that Peter Wimsey would surely have deprecated, I decided that since Shrewsbury College was in fact Somerville, and since Sayers had gone to Somerville, if I too went to Somerville I too could become a writer.

I passed the Entrance exam and got in. Sitting in the college library, I realized I could stay up all night reading if I so wished. Boyfriends would come and go, but I would become a feminist, a socialist. This was my desired *nuit blanche*. I had found my true love.

MICHÈLE ROBERTS has written novels, short stories, poetry, memoir and artist's books. She is half-English and half-French and lives in London.

Hitting the Nail on the Head

YSENDA MAXTONE GRAHAM

1. Jan Struther, the well-known and successful writer, lecturer, radio performer etc. (with a subdivision called Jan Struther, the much-too-little-known and really pretty terrific serious poet whose depth and brilliance will only really be appreciated by a discerning literary public after she is dead!)

That 'item no. 1' was the first on a list concocted by my grandmother Jan Struther in a letter to her brother Douglas in 1951. Jan was famous as the creator of Mrs Miniver, the Chelsea housewife (partly based on her) whose cheerful wifely and motherly common sense had enchanted readers of *The Times* in 1938–9, before being snapped up by MGM for the film based on the character, *Mrs Miniver*, in 1942.

When Jan wrote that letter, six years after the end of the war, Douglas was suffering from depression, a condition with which Jan was all too familiar. In order to cheer him up and show her empathy, she listed all the roles, public and private, that she was trying to juggle.

Well, that hopeful prediction about being recognized as a 'pretty terrific serious poet' hasn't happened, and she died 65 years ago. If you count hymns as poems, which I think I do, because George Herbert's certainly are, the only poem for which Jan is famous is her hymn 'Lord of all hopefulness', written for Percy Dearmer's *Songs of Praise* in 1930. It's a top wedding and funeral choice, a fact that illustrates Jan's ability to entwine happiness and sadness.

Jan would be surprised at the success of that hymn, as she wasn't a churchgoer and thought she would only be remembered for Mrs Miniver. One of the roles she mentioned in that list to her brother was the expatriate Jan, now living in the USA, who longed to hear a peal of bells from an English church tower, 'so long as she wouldn't have to go to the service'.

I wish I could help her with her bid for Poets' Corner but I fear it's too late. As she herself wrote,

> Like rays once shed
>   By a spent star
> The words of a dead
>   Poet are,
> That through bleak space
>   Unchecked fly on,
> Though heart, hand, face
>   To dust are gone,
> And you who read
>   Shall only guess
> What thorn-sharp need,
>   What loneliness,
> What love, lust, dream,
>   Shudder or sigh
> Lit the long beam
>   That meets your eye.

The instantly noticeable thing about Jan's poems is that you can understand them. I worry that this means they can't be very good. Reading English at university in the 1980s, I was indoctrinated into the T. S. Eliot-inspired theory that for a poem to be great it has to be difficult, or at least ambiguous.

Jan's poems aren't difficult to understand. They just express a refreshing thought in a concise, usually rhyming way. For example, this thought about the three stages of falling in love:

> When to this fire I held a taper,
> First flared the impressionable paper;

I watched the paper, as I stood,
Kindle the more enduring wood;
And from the wood a vanguard stole
To set alight the steadfast coal.
So, when I love, the first afire
Is body, with its quick desire;
Then in a little while I find
The flame has crept into my mind –
Till steadily, sweetly burns the whole
Bright conflagration of my soul.

Here are some of her thoughts, in her first collected book of poems, *Betsinda Dances* (1931). London love can be just as romantic as country love in spite of the less romantic backdrop. I'm stuck in my relationship with you, strangled by the cobwebs of habit. It's better to be madly in love and not loved back than vice versa. King Midas could make gold but he couldn't make a buttercup. A beloved person has died: let us forget her rather than remember her, as remembrance is too painful. Life goes too fast but the days go too slowly. Our love affair was too brief and now lies dead, but don't bury it because it might flicker back into life. Hooray, I'm out of love: I'm free, but 'tortured, blind, mad, caged', I was once a god. Each of those thoughts is fashioned into a short poem that rhymes and scans.

I wonder what Jan's husband Tony thought of some of those poems, especially the ones about being trapped in a dull marriage and about having brief love affairs. They were still madly in love in 1931, I'm pretty sure. It was only two years later that everything started to go wrong when Tony got too interested in golf. She dedicates the book to him, with a charming bit of doggerel, addressing the question of whether a happy person can write good poetry:

For only in two kinds of earth
Can poets bring their songs to birth –
In sorrow's rich and heavy clay,

Or else (and here's the rarer way)
Out of the loamy light caress
Of an abundant happiness.

From the early 1920s Jan started writing verses for *Punch* under the pseudonym 'Jan', illustrated by E. H. Shepard. They were published by Methuen in 1932 in *Sycamore Square and Other Verses*, and are now highly collectible, not for the poems but for the Shepard illustrations. But you couldn't have one without the other. These are definitely verses, not poetry: short-lined rhyming couplets about life in a London square (based on Wellington Square, the cul-de-sac in Chelsea where Jan and Tony lived with their children, bicycles, tricycles, nanny, muffin man, bobby on the beat and so on).

Ernest H. Shepard, 'Sycamore Square'

In the same vein, Jan and E. H. Shepard produced *The Modern Struwwelpeter* as a Christmas book for 1935: cautionary verses inspired by the foibles of Jan's own children and their cousins. From which I still quote to myself, when in the role of 'Bank of Mum and Dad',

Children, nowadays (it's funny)
Seem to think one's *made* of money.

When the *Mrs Miniver* phenomenon took off in 1939 and 1940, Jan's new publishers, Chatto & Windus, begged her for any other work. She showed them the poems she'd been writing through the 1930s, most of them published in the *Spectator* and the *London Mercury*, and they snapped them up, publishing *The Glass Blower and Other Poems* in 1940. In contrast to *Mrs Miniver*, which became a national and international bestseller, this book of poems went largely unnoticed.

It was here that we see the beginnings of Jan's depressive side. The opening lines of this poem couldn't be further away from the light-heartedness of her Shepard collaborations:

> Bankrupt of joy, who was once rich in it,
> Must drop pretence at last, no longer hide
> Behind drawn blinds, rooms ravished by distraint;
> Swallow his pride,
> And openly admit
> His fortune spent.

There is ambiguity here: Tony and Jan, spendthrift and broke, had been forced to move out of their family house. But 'bankrupt of joy' (the sprung rhythm reminds me of Gerald Manley Hopkins) was a state of mind as well, and one she would increasingly come to know.

The great love affair of her life had not even started when she submitted that volume. There's one poem about two lovers who, knowing that their love is a blind alley, a cul-de-sac, must go slowly and endlessly retrace their steps in order to cheat themselves into contentment. This was a premonition, because Jan would soon be doing exactly this with Dolf Placzek, the Viennese Jewish refugee with whom she fell in love in November 1939. Their love seemed like a cul-de-sac, but thanks to a succession of miracles – his getting a visa for the USA and her being sent there too as an unofficial ambassadress for Britain for the war years – it turned out not to be. A new level of ecstasy and desolation now enters her poems: this one, for example, about the Cinderella-effect brought on by the presence or absence of the beloved:

> While you are here Beloved, while you are here,
>   Happiness clothes me round like a golden gown.
> The young men smile, and turn their heads, and stare,
>   As I step light-footed through the enchanted town.
> But when you are gone, Beloved, when you are gone,
>   The slippers of glass will vanish, and the golden gown;
> And no one will look at the rags that I have on
>   As I walk with feet of lead through the desolate town.

Through the war years, travelling around America across 'snowy wastes of illimitable prairie' to give lectures to vast audiences in her role as Mrs Miniver, Jan wrote poems in her notebook as she gazed out of train windows. Two of her poems attained recognition in high places. One, 'The American Way of Life', contrasted the real, deep, noble, brave, wise America of the Founding Fathers with the small-mindedness of isolationists. She dared to send a copy to Eleanor Roosevelt, who wrote straight back, asking for permission for the President to read the poem in his next broadcast. Jan was invited to stay at the White House in July 1943, and it was here, I think, that she reached the high-water mark of her success. I love this poem about high-water marks, in *The Glass Blower*:

> This knowledge at least is spared us: we cannot tell
> When any given tide on the heart's shore
> Comes to the full.
> The crown-wave makes no signal, does not cry –
> 'This is the highest. Mark it with a bright shell.
> It will be reached no more.'
> Few could endure
> That knowledge, and not die.
> It is better to be unsure.

The other pivotal poem was 'A Londoner in New England, 1940'. This is an elegy for the bricks of London and a tribute to the city's spirit, written in America during the Blitz. Jan describes how she lived in London as a child, brought up on the nursery rhymes 'London's burning, London's burning' and 'London Bridge is falling down', and how now, far, far away, she can hear a voice 'calmly reciting what the night has done'.

> I think, 'London's burning, London's burning.'
> I think, 'London Bridge is falling down.'
> Then something wiser than thought says, 'Heart, take comfort:
> Buildings and bridges do not make a town.
>
> A city is greater than its bricks and mortar;
> It is greater than tower or palace, church or hall:
> A city's as great as the people that live there.
> You know those people. How can London fall?'

If only the BBC had recorded and kept hold of things in those days. That poem was read aloud by Celia Johnson in the Royal Albert Hall on Thanksgiving Day 1944, at the United Thanksgiving Service. I want to hear a crackly version of Celia Johnson reading it: the great Celia, wife of Peter Fleming whose very idea it was that Jan should write about 'an ordinary sort of woman, rather like yourself' for the Court Page of *The Times*, thus bringing Mrs Miniver to birth.

Straight after the last line had been read, the orchestra swept into Elgar's *Cockaigne Overture*, and Churchill spoke: 'We are moving forward surely, steadily, irresistibly and perhaps with God's aid, swiftly, towards victorious peace.'

As for Jan's epitaph (and ours), we can take our choice: the dark side or the light side of Looking Back at Life. The last poem she ever wrote, as she sailed away from England in 1951 for the final time, and soon to be diagnosed with terminal cancer, of which she died aged 52, was one about the seven days of de-creation, that are the essence of saying a final goodbye. The bleakness of that poem shows Jan to be someone who can plumb the depths of despair.

Or you can choose as her (and our) epitaph the poem 'Biography' at the end of *Betsinda Dances*:

> One day my life will end; and lest
>   Some whim should prompt you to review it,
> Let her who knows the subject best
>   Tell you the shortest way to do it:
> Then say, 'Here lies one doubly blest.'
>   Say, 'She was happy.' Say, 'She knew it.'

YSENDA MAXTONE GRAHAM reviews books for *The Times* and the *Daily Mail*, and writes a monthly column in *Country Life*. Her next book, *British Summertime Begins*, about British childhood summers, will be published in 2020.

Jan Struther, *Betsinda Dances* (1931), *Sycamore Square and Other Verses* (1932, illus. E. H. Shepard), *The Modern Struwwelpeter* (1935, illus. E. H. Shepard) and *The Glass Blower and Other Poems* (1940) are out of print but we can obtain second-hand copies.

The full story of Ysenda's grandmother is told by her in *The Real Mrs Miniver*, available as a Slightly Foxed Edition (subscribers: UK & Eire £17, Overseas £19; non-subscribers: UK & Eire £18.50, Overseas £20.50). All prices include post and packing. Copies may be ordered by post (53 Hoxton Square, London N1 6PB), by phone (020 7033 0258) or via our website www.foxedquarterly.com.

The Twilight Hour

MIRANDA SEYMOUR

My mother died last year. Aged 94, she went without pain, fear or regret. The loss was ours, not hers: the loss of that protective sense of the generation that stands between us and our own ending; the loss, too, of that indefinable ease bred by a lifetime of familiarity with a shared past.

Thinking about her as I walked across flat fields in February, towards the end of day, I watched the darkness settle across the fields, leaving, faraway, a single bright patch of gold, an unattainable kingdom created by the low rays of the sinking sun. Twilight – the subject of Peter Davidson's meditative and beautiful book *The Last of the Light* (2015) – is the moment when nature seems to embrace and enfold us within herself. The ache of bereavement adjusts and resolves itself into acceptance: an understanding that twilight is itself a resignation, a dying of the day, from which renewal arises.

Many of the favourite books so wonderfully evoked and reclaimed in *Slightly Foxed* have previously been subjected to a lifetime of affectionate rereading. But I had never heard of Peter Davidson until the friend with whom I was out on that February stroll chose to send me this singular book. Since then, I have tracked down and devoured three other similarly poetic works by the same author. All seem to have been written while Davidson was living in what he calls 'a remote and exceptional part of Scotland' – just north of the Cairngorms in the Eastern Highlands. This is where he stands at the

Peter Davidson, *The Last of the Light* (2015)
Reaktion Books · Pb · 208pp · £14.95 · ISBN 9781780235103

opening of *The Last of the Light*, 'on shadowed slopes, on the bare shoulder of the hill, outside the old boundaries of Empire, on the far margin of Europe'.

Davidson's book offers us a series of intense, lyrical and surprisingly moving meditations on landscapes, buildings and mythical settings, as seen at the close of day through the eyes of painters and writers. *The Last of the Light* is a spellbinding exploration of that haunted moment of transition, either on some particular evening or in the history of the civilizations through which Davidson effortlessly roams. Again and again we find ourselves confronting the familiar with fresh eyes, noticing the tiny but significant details that he brings to the fore and quickens into life.

The engravings of Samuel Palmer provide a fine example of his method. Briefly, he tells the story of the Victorian artist's sad life: a wretched marriage; the loss of a beloved eldest son. Nine years before his death in 1881, Palmer found solace in illustrating Virgil's *Eclogues*. Davidson describes these drawings as 'his last place of retreat from a hostile present'. 'The Homeward Star' – Palmer's representation of Virgil's celebrated account of the approach of dusk – looks back for comfort and inspiration, Davidson suggests, to happier times when a sturdy young artist went wandering through summer fields all evening long. Years later, recognizing how much of the world of his youth had vanished, Palmer recast Virgil's hospitable little homes as industrial chimney-stacks, reminders of a business-like age in which the artist was never at ease. Behind them, heavy woods cluster beneath the blackly medieval peaks of Virgil's shadow-shrouded mountains. Melancholy hovers, as if with folded wings. But Davidson gently draws our attention upwards – to a sky palely brightened by Palmer's beloved motifs of an evening star and a sleeping crescent moon – and then downward again, to where an almost invisible group of shepherds has gathered to chat around a simply laid table. Light glows down upon this tiny rustic party from the interior of a woodland cabin, their refuge from the night.

Davidson points to a similar group in 'The Bellman', Palmer's 1879 illustration for Milton's 'Il Penseroso'. Here, the sinister, long-coated figure of the bell-ringer stalks the dusky street of an Italianate village. To one side sits another merry little group of evening diners. Sadness and reassurance mingle in the twilight, evoking in another of Davidson's apt quotations what the art historian Erwin Panofsky called 'the feeling of evening silently settling over the world'.

Occasionally, Davidson steps forward to introduce his own experiences of what Parisians call 'the blue hour', that blink-and-it's-gone moment in the evening when – before our light-polluting cities banished such distinctions – Nabokov could record the merging of a

gradual and dual blue
As night unites the viewer with the view.

Recalling one such evening in August at his Scottish home, he describes the protracted enjoyment of sitting with guests in a dusk-mantled garden. Candles glimmer in the grass. The house lights brighten as the sky loses its first evening brilliance. Walking with his wife towards the shadowed trees and the river beyond, he turns with a moment's wistfulness to look back at their younger, oblivious guests, 'to where they sit under the firefly lanterns in the last of the light. We are hearing the fall of water they cannot yet hear.'

This poignant sense of the fugitive moment and the coming to an end of things haunts Davidson's strange and magical book. Intelligence, unexpected insights, and the recognition that he is always writing about more than the transient delight of a long summer evening, succeed in holding melancholy at bay.

Moving from Palmer's wistful minor key to a thundering major chord, Davidson suggests that Europe has been living in an era of twilight ever since the passing of the great civilizations from which it was born.

Through the centuries, European culture has, to some degree, felt itself to be an after-culture, a broken culture of shadow and echo. All times after the lost, bright world of Greece and Rome are 'twilight' . . . The age of gold declines to our age of iron, and exile and shadow are the undersong of our histories. Our own age too can be readily seen as a spoiled and darkening one, littered with a tidewrack of falling monuments to the hopes of post-war Europe.

He shares Palmer's view of twilight as a refuge from an unfriendly present, mourning the fact that our present way of life has almost succeeded in extinguishing the subtle hues of each day's transition into night. Twilight brings a moment that has, over the centuries, been celebrated by artists, poets and naturalists. Davidson's natural affinity is with writers such as Ruskin and Gerard Manley Hopkins who anxiously recorded the dramatic effects of a changing climate upon the evening sky.

To Davidson, the whole of the nineteenth century lies enfolded within the exquisitely coffined sadness that descends at dusk. His descriptions repeatedly remind us of the 'melancholy, belated lives' evoked by John Atkinson Grimshaw's sepia and gold paintings of city evenings. The pollution-obsessed Ruskin noticed in them only 'the smoke-drifts that blanch the sunlight', and Davidson shares his distress. One entire page of his book is devoted to the image of a carefully preserved glass bottle in which, like mud, a puddle of the dense black rain that fell across Lancashire in 1884 has been sealed up for close on a century and a half.

Exploring the dark side of twilight, Davidson takes as an example the painter James Pryde ('the Edgar Allan Poe of Painting'), master of haunted rooms and scenes of violence. Pryde's rooms lie buried in darkness, lit only by 'a small spillage of illumination – thus the moment of depiction is always a twilight moment'.

Davidson quotes G. K. Chesterton's marvellous description of the hour when darkness descends upon the London inhabited by his

F. L. Griggs, *Duntisbourne Rouse*, 1927, etching

amiable detective, Father Brown: 'that thrilling mood and moment, when the eyes of a great city, like the eyes of a cat, begin to flame in the dark'. More ghostly evocations he finds in a letter from William Maxwell, describing for his friend Sylvia Townsend Warner the moment on an Irish country evening when it is possible to register an 'almost darkness that is still a kind of light' as a moment in which 'the supernatural is not at all improbable'.

Warner knew just what he meant. Davidson cites the moment when Lolly Willowes, the eponymous heroine of one of Warner's most beguiling novels, strays from a comfortable fireside to seek out the excitements of a deserted countryside at twilight. 'Looking into the well, she watched the reflected sky grow dimmer, and when she raised her eyes the gathering darkness of the landscape surprised her. The time had come.'

*

Caspar David Friedrich's wonderful painting of *The Evening Star*; Robert Louis Stevenson's enraptured first glimpse of his future wife through a lamplit window at dusk; the 'unconsoled twilight' in which Sebald's great novel *Austerlitz* gradually approaches its conclusion; the hours of patient preparation invested in Sargent's glorious painting of children lighting lanterns in a riverside garden, captured at the moment when the flowers and faces of *Carnation, Lily, Lily, Rose* are about to be touched by evening's first shadows; the unexpected link between that famous image and *Edwin Drood*'s Mr Crisparkle, lilting out the Victorian ballad from which Sargent took his haunting title – Davidson offers us moments of discovery and startling connection on almost every page.

The Last of the Light transforms the subject of twilight into a constantly rewarding study of art and history, entwined with observations of the seasonal changes to an abiding Scottish landscape. That barren landscape perfectly mirrors the implicit sadness in Davidson's book, that moment when – as with each bright day – 'the year hurries down towards the dark'.

MIRANDA SEYMOUR is a biographer and critic.

At War with Churchill

ANTHONY LONGDEN

A lonely senior army officer takes up his pen and writes a dedication
to his wife in the flyleaf of a virgin notebook:

> This book is not intended to be a diary of events, although it
> may contain references to my daily life. It is intended to be a
> record of my thoughts and impressions such as I would have
> discussed them with you had we been together . . .

The date is 28 September 1939. The author cannot know that what
he will record in this 15-shilling notebook – and the many that follow
it over the next six years – will become an astonishing first-hand
account of Britain's darkest hours, and a vivid, often harrowing portrait of one of its greatest leaders. For this is an extraordinary soldier,
General Sir Alan Brooke, later Field Marshal Lord Alanbrooke, destined to become Churchill's right-hand man as head of the British
armed forces, and broker of the Grand Alliance with Roosevelt and
Stalin. Yet despite the pivotal role he played, his name is still compar-
atively little known.

Twentieth-century military diaries are a mixed bag, and big names
are no guarantee of readability. General 'Pug' Ismay was Churchill's
military assistant during the war, but that didn't prevent him from
producing a memoir of paralysing tedium. Field Marshal Montgomery's memoirs are worth a go, but only because his legendary

Field Marshal Lord Alanbrooke, *War Diaries, 1939–1945* (2001) · Eds. Alex
Danchev & Daniel Todman
Weidenfeld & Nicolson · Pb · 816pp · £19.99 · ISBN 9781842125267

ego rampages across every page, almost making the book a comic masterpiece.

I much prefer honest, more human accounts – Spike Milligan's side-splitting though often poignant tales of his wartime army service perhaps, John Hackett's *I Was a Stranger* (SF Edition no. 25) or Anthony Rhodes's *Sword of Bone* (SF Edition no. 35). But in my view, the Rolls-Royce of the bunch is Alanbrooke. His candid diaries are unparalleled gems.

Even so, their first published incarnations did not serve them well. An ill-fated collaboration with the historian Arthur Bryant produced *The Turn of the Tide* (1957) and *Triumph in the West* (1959). Bryant seems not to have had the stomach for the job, bowdlerizing the diaries and rendering them anodyne and dull. Fortunately, in 2001, the historians Alex Danchev and Daniel Todman produced an unexpurgated version that also included comments added by Alanbrooke in the 1950s. The result sparkles, and its warmth and humanity lift it into the first rank.

The diaries were born out of the loneliness and isolation of high military office. So while they allow Alanbrooke to vent his spleen as near-intolerable pressure mounts, they also offer the reader a portrait of fraught working relationships and crushing responsibilities.

It was said the old soldier never intended to publish them. However, he grew increasingly irritated with the release of each successive volume of Churchill's own version of events, *The Second World War*, which appeared between 1948 and 1954. Alanbrooke felt the great man had been ungenerous to those around him, and that his own singular effort had been relegated to little more than a footnote. Even so, he sent Churchill a copy of his diaries when they came out, with a generous personal inscription on the flyleaf reaffirming his 'unbounded admiration, profound respect, and deep affection'.

Churchill replied with one icy paragraph of thanks.

In many ways Alanbrooke was an outsider, something that makes his rise through the ranks all the more remarkable. Although of Irish aristocratic stock he had been born in the Pyrenees in 1883 and spent the first sixteen years of his life in France. He was a wiry, stylish man with strong Continental looks – black hair slicked to his scalp, a long, tanned face, a regally beaky nose, a neatly trimmed moustache and small, berry-dark eyes.

Alanbrooke's career had taken off as a result of his decisive leadership of II Corps of the British Expeditionary Force in the lead-up to the miraculous evacuation from Dunkirk – a feat that ought to have been impossible. He was dismayed to be sent straight back over the Channel in the vain hope of rallying the French. He knew it was a hopeless task, but characteristically he did his best until time ran out and the country surrendered. His sound military judgement and cool head did not go unnoticed. The newly installed Prime Minister wanted him as his Commander-in-Chief Home Forces.

> When I thump the table and push my face towards him, what does he do? Thumps the table harder and glares back at me. I know these Brookes – stiff-necked Ulstermen, and there's no one worse to deal with than that!

Churchill was joking when he wrote that, but in the years ahead he frequently found himself eyeball-to-eyeball with Alanbrooke in a tempestuous exchange of views.

The C-in-C Home role was a tall order. Invasion was imminent, and meeting that threat was Alanbrooke's principal responsibility. Unsurprisingly, he was racked with anxiety. It is this that gives his diaries their power. The entry for 19 July 1940 is typical:

> I find it hard to realize fully the responsibility I am assuming. I only pray to God that I may be capable of carrying out the job. The idea of failure at this stage of the war is too ghastly to

contemplate. I know that you will be with me in praying to
God that he may give me the necessary strength and guidance.

The Battle of Britain was already raging, with the Luftwaffe
pounding south-east England. Home defence had been a rather lick-
and-stick affair, poorly equipped and chaotic, with even the most
basic tools of war – rifles, ammunition, anti-tank guns, tanks and
armoured cars – in woefully short supply. Alanbrooke set to work,
lobbying hard for the equipment he needed, rigorously training
troops, devising innovative defensive tactics, overhauling the command structure and dramatically improving communications.

Fortunately, the invasion never came, but Alanbrooke's energy had
impressed Churchill, who now wanted him for the top job – Chief
of the Imperial General Staff (CIGS). If the Home defence role had
been a challenge, the sheer magnitude of this new task was off the
scale. Ultimate responsibility for prosecution of the entire war placed
on the shoulders of one man was one thing. But there was another
hurdle – he had to work with Churchill:

> I had seen enough of him . . . his impetuous nature, his gam-
> bler's spirit, and his determination to follow his own selected
> path at all costs, to realize fully what I was faced with.

Alanbrooke assumed his new role on 1 December 1941. Within a
week, the Japanese had brought the United States into the war with
their attack on Pearl Harbor, and the new CIGS's organizational
headaches instantly became global.

Things rapidly got worse. On 10 December 1941, Alanbrooke
arrived at the War Office to be told that the Japanese had sunk the
British battleships *Prince of Wales* and *Repulse.*

> This . . . puts us in a very serious position for the prosecution
> of the war. It means that from Africa eastwards to America
> through the Indian Ocean and the Pacific, we have lost com-

mand of the sea. This affects reinforcements to the Middle East, India, Burma, the Far East, Australia and New Zealand!

Not only did he have to deal with the day-to-day business of the military machine, he now also had to play an integral part in handling international diplomacy among the allies that led to the so-called Grand Alliance. The relationship with the United States had to be finessed and plans of action agreed upon. Eggshell-delicate negotiations with the Soviet Union followed. Despite what was at stake, these produced some of the most amusing passages in the diaries. Alanbrooke's encounters with Stalin and his generals are marvellously described, especially his accounts of formal dinners at the Kremlin, where Soviet generals were apt to slide slowly under the table as the evening wore on:

> I was in dread of this banquet all day and shuddered at the idea of having to spend the evening dodging the effects of vodka . . . During the first hour we got through at least a dozen toasts. Luckily, I had a jug of water in front of me, and when I was not being watched I filled up my glass with water instead of vodka . . . In front of me amongst the many fish dishes was a small suckling pig covered with a blanket of white sauce. He had a black truffle eye and an orange peel mouth. He was never eaten, and as the evening slipped by his black eye remained fixed on me, and the orange peel mouth developed a sardonic smile! I can still see that pig now if I shut my eyes.

Alanbrooke recognized Stalin as 'an outstanding man but not an attractive one', describing his 'cold, crafty, dead face', and finding no difficulty in imagining him sending people to their doom without turning a hair.

As the war progresses the diaries steadily fill with details of battle after battle – not just with the Germans and the Japanese, but also between Alanbrooke and Churchill. It was not unusual to see the

Prime Minister sulking, crying with rage or shaking his fist in some-one's face. His sarcasm was also hard to take. Alanbrooke's notes for February 1942 give a typical example:

> He came out continually with remarks such as: 'Have you not got a single general in that army who can win battles? Have none of them any ideas? Must we continually lose battles in this way?' etc etc. Such remarks lowered the confidence of other ministers in the efficiency of the army, and could be nothing but detrimental to the present crisis.

Despite many more morale-sapping blows, the Allies gradually began to gain the upper hand. Churchill's failing health left him increasingly fractious and exhausted. He was losing his grasp on detail, and often on reality. On 6 July 1944 Alanbrooke wrote:

> At 10 pm we had a frightful meeting with Winston which lasted until 2 am!! It was quite the worst we have had with him. He was very tired . . . he had tried to recuperate with drink. As a result he was in a maudlin, bad tempered, drunken mood, ready to take offence at anything, suspicious of everybody, and in a highly vindictive mood against the Americans. In fact so vindictive that his whole outlook on strategy was warped.

By September, things were no better. Alanbrooke was by now ser-iously concerned that Churchill's behaviour risked damaging the all-important relationship with the American commanders in co-ordinating the final liberation of Europe. After a particularly bad meeting, he wrote:

> He was again in a most unpleasant mood. Produced the most ridiculous arguments . . . He knows no details, has only got half the picture in his mind, talks absurdities and makes my blood boil to listen to his nonsense. I find it hard to remain civil. And the wonderful thing is that ¾ of the population of the world

Alanbrooke's entry for 6 June 1944

imagine that Winston Churchill is one of the Strategists of History, a second Marlborough, and the other ¼ have no conception what a public menace he is and has been throughout this war! It is far better that the world should never know and never suspect the feet of clay of that otherwise superhuman being. Without him England was lost for a certainty, with him England has been on the verge of disaster time and time again . . . Never have I admired and despised a man simultaneously to the same extent. Never have such opposite extremes been combined in the same human being.

However, it is clear from his subsequent footnotes that he was haunted by the rawness of his original diary entries on Churchill and was keen to place them in context:

> On reading these diaries I have repeatedly felt ashamed of the abuse I had poured on him, especially during the latter years. It must, however, be remembered that my diary was the safety valve and only outlet for all my pent-up feelings. Feelings that had been engendered through friction generated from prolonged contacts of very tired individuals.

He admitted he had failed to make adequate allowance for Churchill's ill health, when the Prime Minister had suffered repeated bouts of pneumonia and other ailments, but he was generous in his final assessment of their time together:

> I shall always look back on the years I worked with him as some of the most difficult and trying ones in my life. For all that, I thank God that I was given an opportunity of working alongside of such a man, and of having my eyes opened to the fact that occasionally such supermen exist on this earth.

If you are only able to read one military diary, do make it this one. There really is none better.

ANTHONY LONGDEN has been a journalist for 35 years, 22 of them spent as a local newspaper editor and senior executive. Now a specialist partner in a crisis-handling firm, he is also a director of the Colne Valley Regional Park, the first real taste of countryside to the west of London.

Lost in the Fens

JULIE WELCH

Should you really never judge a book by its cover? Had I gone along with that dictum years ago I would not have happened upon Edmund Crispin. Shameful though it is to admit it, I was attracted not by the name of the author – unknown to me – but by a Penguin Crime jacket. Its green and cream design caught my eye at an Amnesty International book sale in the church opposite our house. Our dining-room had recently been redecorated, and I judged *Frequent Hearses* would, suitably displayed, tone with the colour scheme.

First published in 1950, this was a 1987 paperback edition, apparently untouched. Not for long; once I'd handed over £1.50 I couldn't resist a look inside, and by the seventh sentence I was entranced:

> The cross-country journey is prolonged and tedious, involving four changes – at stations of progressively diminishing size and increasing antiquity, so that the effect is of witnessing a dramatized History of the Railways in reverse . . .

This was crime fiction with a difference. But who was Edmund Crispin? A brief blurb told me that his real name was Bruce Montgomery; 'Edmund Crispin' was borrowed from a character in one of Michael Innes's Inspector Appleby novels, *Hamlet, Revenge!*

Edmund Crispin, *The Case of the Gilded Fly* (1944), *Holy Disorders* (1945), *The Moving Toyshop* (1946), *Swan Song* (1947), *Love Lies Bleeding* (1948), *Buried for Pleasure* (1948), *Frequent Hearses* (1950), *The Long Divorce* (1951) and *The Glimpses of the Moon* (1977) are available in paperback, mostly under the Collins Crime Club imprint at £8.99 each.

As well as writing he had been a composer of film scores and concert music, and until his death in 1978 lived in Devon 'in a quiet corner whose exploitation and development he did his utmost to oppose'.

I loved the way this author wrote and wondered why I had never heard of him. 'Forgotten Authors', a 2008 piece in the *Independent* by Christopher Fowler, supplied an answer: 'Nobody wants to be thought of as vanished, but shelf-life is fleeting.' Crispin, one of Fowler's Forgotten, was 'an important critic and editor but best of all he wrote the Gervase Fen books, 11 dazzling, joyous volumes, all but one of which were produced between 1944 and 1951'.

I trawled second-hand bookshops and later the Internet for further Fens. The protagonist of *Frequent Hearses* and Crispin's eight other novels (there are also two collections of short stories) is an Oxford professor who moonlights as an amateur detective. *The Moving Toyshop* (1946) describes him as 'a tall, lanky man, about forty years of age, with a cheerful, lean, ruddy, clean-shaven face. His dark hair, sedulously plastered down with water, stuck up in spikes at the crown.'

He has children and, according to *The Case of the Gilded Fly* (1944), a wife: 'a plain, spectacled, sensible little woman incongruously called Dolly'. He sports 'an extraordinary hat', headgear which is referred to in subsequent books though the nature of its singularity is never explained. He drives a small red sports car, 'exceptionally strident and dissolute-looking', with *Lily Christine III* painted in white across the bonnet, collects insects in his wardrobe – part of the dénouement of *Holy Disorders* (1945) – quotes the White Rabbit ('Oh my ears and whiskers!') in times of stress or astonishment, and is 'habitually rude to everyone; it was a consequence . . . of his monstrous and excessive vitality'. In other words, an overgrown, very intelligent schoolboy.

As for Crispin (I'll keep calling him that; it's easier than rechristening him Montgomery), he was born in 1921 to an Ulsterman father – a civil servant – and a Scottish mother, his upbringing being what he described as 'conventionally middle class . . . For all its limitations, decent *bourgeoisism* seems to me not at all a bad or unreasonable code to live by – or to write by, either.' At St John's College, Oxford, he took a BA in Modern Languages and was, for two years, its organ scholar and choirmaster, keeping a grand piano in his room.

> I must have seen [him] on my first morning in St John's in 1941 coming out of his staircase in the front quad to go to the bath-house [recalled Kingsley Amis, a friend and contemporary]. This man, along with an indefinable and daunting air of maturity, had a sweep of wavy auburn hair, a silk dressing gown in some non-primary shade and a walk that looked eccentric and mincing.

The Noël Coward-ish affectations were self-inflicted, the distinctive gait not so; Amis later discovered that it was caused by a congenital deformity of both feet.

According to another friend, Philip Larkin, to whom *The Moving Toyshop* is dedicated:

> He was lazy but with a far more brilliant brain than I. He was expected to get a First by nearly everyone, and the responsibility weighed on him, driving him to the bar of the Randolph, but rarely to his desk and books.

And – Larkin again – 'Beneath this formidable exterior, however, Bruce had unexpected depths of frivolity.' To which end, he badgered Victor Gollancz with novels, all of which bounced back until *The Case of the Gilded Fly*. Written in the Easter vacation of 1943, it was a locked-room mystery inspired by John Dickson Carr's *The Crooked Hinge*.

Over the next few years, Crispin produced book after book like a magician releasing doves from the sleeve of his gown. Characters in *The Moving Toyshop* include a student, Hoskins, who is 'large, raw-boned and melancholy, a little like a Thurber dog'. There are funny, silly, literary jokes; at one tense point in the proceedings Fen initiates a game of 'Detestable Characters in Fiction' – step forward 'Lady Chatterley and that gamekeeper fellow', 'Those awful gabblers, Beatrice and Benedick' and 'Almost everybody in Dostoevsky'. I won't spoil the dénouement for you, but it adumbrates the climactic sequence of Alfred Hitchcock's *Strangers on a Train*. Crispin received no credit for it, of course.

The Moving Toyshop is meant to be his masterpiece, even if, as one exasperated reviewer put it at the time, 'Heaven help you if you're expecting detection.' My favourite, though, is *Love Lies Bleeding* (1948), set in a boys' public school. Crispin maintained that his knowledge of criminal behaviour was attributable to his first post-graduate job, that of a master at Shrewsbury. It is the only work of crime fiction ever to have made me hoot with laughter. This is mainly due to Mr Merrythought, an ancient, forbidding bloodhound who effects his entrance by dribbling and trying to climb on a table.

The books have wit, descriptive power, earthiness and exuberant farce of the comedy car-chase variety. *Buried for Pleasure* (1948) delivers a rectory-dwelling poltergeist and an escaped lunatic. In *The Glimpses of the Moon* (1977) a pylon is virtually a comic character. It is called the Pisser. I will leave it at that. Bonus points, as far as I am concerned, are won by the absence of soppy love scenes and hanky-panky that commonly hold up the action in crime fiction. Characters fall in love via the *coup de foudre* and are generally on the way to the altar within a fortnight. There are no jeremiads for the deceased, simply Fen's dispassionate curiosity. The clues to solve the puzzle are there but you are often having too much fun to spot them.

By the time he was 32, Crispin had written eight novels as well as twenty-eight musical compositions. *Frequent Hearses* is the antepenultimate Fen and, though equally amusing, has lost the giggly vitality of *The Moving Toyshop*. *The Long Divorce*, which followed in 1951, was the last for twenty-six years.

It was The Case of the Disappearing Detective Novelist. Where did Edmund Crispin of the Gervase Fen novels go? For a time he wrote film scores; the fact that between 1958 and 1962 they included six for the *Carry On* series – *Sergeant, Nurse, Teacher, Constable, Regardless* and *Cruising* – simply adds to the zany charm. And after that? Writing in 1991, Douglas G. Greene, in his introduction to *The Case of the Gilded Fly*, quotes Crispin as explaining, 'I lay fallow for the most part, drinking rather too heavily and writing little . . .'

In 1967 he replaced Julian Symons, president of the Detective Club, as the *Sunday Times*'s crime fiction reviewer, reading an average of forty books a month for five years. A price was paid for his conscientiousness. 'To read a book a day for you – which is what it amounts to – does leave one in increasing ignorance of what is going on elsewhere in the literary world,' he complained mildly to his editor.

To learn more, I visited the Newsroom at the British Library and armed myself with microfilm of every *Sunday Times* for 1967. A random choice, November to December, proved lucky; here, on the review pages, was Edmund Crispin making his debut under the headline 'Criminal Records' (I bet he thought that one up himself). Few journalists disclosed details of their personal lives back then, so from that point of view I was none the wiser about the missing years, though reading his elliptical, brisk, compressed prose was a pleasure. I was left with the impression of a kind, decent person who wrote without malice, his reviews guided by the old adage, 'If you can't say something nice, don't say anything at all.'

'Marvellous Emma Lathen! I could do with a new book by her every week,' began one review. *Danger: Hospital Zone* by Ursula Curtiss was applauded for its 'First-rate suspense by a dab hand at the job'. Ruth Rendell's talent was spotted early, her third Wexford novel, *Wolf to the Slaughter*, summed up thus:

Interesting station of Sussex police investigating disappearance of a grubby young artist's parsimonious sister. Amusing, well-characterised and well-constructed, with a gratifying surprise ending and some tricksy red herrings to put you at fault from time to time.

I had a sense that Dick Francis's *Blood Sport* was not quite his cup of tea but he politely commended it. I could find only one scathing review, of a book which is manifestly the antithesis of a Gervase Fen. Perhaps it's best not to name the author or the gimcrack book in which, beneath 'the thin wisecracks, the ohgoddery, the blood-letting and the preposterous erotic stamina lies a dispiriting vacuum'. It must have been very bad indeed.

Was it the *Sunday Times* job that got him writing again? The final full-length Gervase Fen appeared a year before the author's death. It is *The Glimpses of the Moon* (1977), and unlike the Bad Crime Novel that shall remain unnamed, it is a baffling, farcically macabre joy.

JULIE WELCH fell in love with detective fiction at the age of 12, when she discovered Sherlock Holmes. One ambition, so far unfulfilled, is to write a crime novel of her own, but she is the author of eleven books, of which her latest is *The Fleet Street Girls*, to be published in 2020.

Winning on Points

JACQUELINE WILSON

The first book I ever bought for myself was *Ballet Shoes* by Noel Streatfeild. I've bought thousands more books since, but *Ballet Shoes* is still a very special favourite. It hasn't been out of print since it was published in 1936. I recently treated myself to a first edition with its rare silver cover (so fragile it generally disintegrated within weeks) but my first copy was a Puffin paperback.

Three girls in white ballet dresses danced across the cover, two on the front and one on the back. They were the three Fossil sisters, Pauline, Petrova and Posy. I didn't yet know anything about them but I knew I wanted to *be* them. I longed to go to ballet lessons and take part in dancing displays wearing a white tutu. Oh, the glamour! But my mother said we couldn't afford it, so I had to make do with dancing at home, pretending my pink bedroom slippers were ballet shoes.

We might not have had money to spare for ballet lessons, but my parents still gave me one shilling pocket money every Saturday. Maths isn't my strong point, but I think that's five modern pence. It seems a pathetically small sum now, but when I was a child it seemed

Noel Streatfeild's *Ballet Shoes* (1936) is available as a Puffin paperback (£6.99 · 352pp · ISBN 9780141359809); *The Whicharts* (1931) is out of print but we can try to obtain second-hand copies.

an agreeably large amount. If I'd been helpful doing the Saturday morning big shop my mother would then let me spend my weekly windfall.

Woolworths was always tempting, with its sweets and its shiny notebooks and its little penny dolls the colour of bubblegum, but I was a passionate reader so I asked Mum if we could go to W. H. Smith. As soon as I spotted *Ballet Shoes* on the Puffin shelf I knew I had to have it. It cost two shillings, so I had to save for another week, which was torture. There was only one copy and I was terrified another child would come along and snaffle it. But there it was, waiting for me the following Saturday, and I took it home ecstatically.

I'd finished it by Sunday teatime. It's a simple enough story: three baby girls are adopted by an eccentric old fossil collector (hence the surname) and left in the care of his great-niece Sylvia. The girls are sent to a stage school run by a formidable Russian called Madame Fidolia. The idea is that they can go on the stage at soon as they are 12 and start earning much-needed money.

All three have great performing potential. Pauline is the prettiest, with pink and white skin and long fair hair. She's a very promising actress. Dark Petrova is the most interesting. Her Russian heritage excites Madame Fidolia, but Petrova isn't at all the sort of girl who likes being on the stage. She wants to be a car mechanic or fly planes. The youngest sister, Posy, is a mischievous little redhead with a gift for dancing, and it soon becomes clear that she's destined to be a ballerina.

Ballet Shoes is in many respects a fairy story with a happily-ever-after ending. Pauline is a great success as an actress and leaves England to become a Hollywood movie star. Petrova is given the chance to fly aeroplanes (very unusual for a young girl in the 1930s). Posy starts training with a prestigious ballet company in Czechoslovakia. Noel Streatfeild ends the story cleverly:

'What different things we are going to do!' said Pauline.

'In such different places,' added Posy.

'I wonder' – Petrova looked up – 'if other girls had to be one of us, which of us they'd choose to be?'

I loved questions like this and pondered them deeply when I was 7. Sometimes I wanted to be Pauline, mostly because I longed to have her long fair hair. I already knew I wanted to be a writer, but I wondered if I could be an actress too. I was good at reading aloud, but I was very quiet in class so my teachers thought I was too shy to act. I was a silent shepherd in old brown curtains in the nativity play, and desperately envied the girl playing Mary in stunning sky blue.

Pauline always has the best parts and is a huge success playing Alice in Wonderland, but it goes to her head. She becomes unbearably conceited and bosses everyone around, especially lording it over her understudy Winifred. I always felt uncomfortable reading about poor Winifred. She's a better actor, dancer and singer than Pauline, but she is plain, comes from a poor home and wears shabby dresses, so is never picked first.

I wanted to be Pauline but knew I was much more a Winifred. She's always haunted me. Perhaps she haunted Noel Streatfeild too, because in a later book, *Curtain Up*, a grown-up Winifred is described as 'a tall, ugly girl with a clever, interesting face'. I still wince at that word 'ugly'.

Would I prefer to be Petrova? I found her intensely interesting, with her passion for cars and planes and her stoic determination to earn money for the family on the stage though she hates performing. She's very much the tomboy sort of heroine current now in children's books – but I didn't really want to *be* her.

That leaves Posy. I loved her independence, and her naughtiness, and her wicked imitations. I admired her talent and wished I could be a brilliant dancer too. But though Posy has a certainty about her that I envied, it also irritated me.

Nowadays I'd choose to be Noel Streatfeild herself rather than any of her characters. Her understanding of children and her ability to make them seem utterly real and convincing was a great gift. The three Fossil sisters, and indeed poor Winifred, are so psychologically sound and so naturally portrayed that *Ballet Shoes* (and most of Streatfeild's other books) remain wonderfully compelling reads.

Times change, of course, and more than eighty years after publication it strikes us as bizarre that the girls are considered poor when they live in London's Cromwell Road in a huge house, and Sylvia, their guardian, employs a nanny and a cook and a maid. However, the detailed description of the girls' daily lives, their plans to pawn the necklaces given them by their Great Uncle Matthew, their pressing need to get a new audition dress, and Petrova's lack of proper presents on her twelfth birthday are all utterly convincing. I savoured the passages about those turquoise, pearl and coral necklaces and the black chiffon velvet audition dress from Harrods.

People often ask which books have influenced me. I know they're asking about writing style, whereas I've always tried to write in my own way – but I've just realized that I happen to be wearing a black velvet dress with a turquoise necklace as I write.

Ballet Shoes was a huge hit when it was first published. When Noel went to Hatchards to buy twelve copies for friends' children she was firmly told that customers were restricted to one copy each. The reviews were splendid: it was described as sparkling, enthralling, delightful and very original. But it wasn't original at all. It was certainly Noel Streatfeild's first children's book, but five years earlier she had written a first novel for adults called *The Whicharts* which is bizarrely similar – and yet incredibly different.

Noel Streatfeild had been an unsuccessful actress, a surprising choice of career for an upper-class vicarage daughter in the 1920s. She lost heart and announced to her sister that she wanted to 'leave the stage and write a best seller'. (She seems to have had Posy's supreme confidence.)

The Whicharts was accepted by the first publisher who saw it – he thought it brilliant and unusual. Reviewers were kind and Noel got admiring letters from famous authors. I was thrilled when I tracked a copy down in a second-hand bookshop. The opening paragraphs were startlingly familiar:

> The Whichart children lived in the Cromwell Road. At that end of it which is furthest away from the Brompton Road, and yet sufficiently near it to be taken to look at the dolls' houses in the Victoria and Albert every wet day, and if not too wet expected to 'save the penny and walk'
>
> Saving the penny and walking was a great feature of their childhood.

Apart from a change of surname the beginning of *Ballet Shoes* is identical. *The Whicharts* and *Ballet Shoes* tell very similar stories – but as I read on I realized that Noel's first book is a much darker, seedier novel than her much-loved children's classic. It wasn't her own idea to write a child's version. A children's editor at J. M. Dent had read and enjoyed *The Whicharts* and asked Noel if she would write a similar children's story about the stage.

Pauline, Petrova and Posy are very similar girls to the three Whicharts, Maimie, Tania and Daisy. (They call themselves 'the Whicharts' because of the Lord's Prayer: 'Our Father Which Art in Heaven'.) The girls are half-sisters. Their father is a Brigadier 'with many honours, and even more mistresses'. Here, great-niece Sylvia in *Ballet Shoes* is Rose, the first of all the mistresses.

The Whicharts is still a very readable novel and well worth tracking down, but I found it disconcerting all the same. It shows the sleazier side of stage life. Even the stage school itself is a grubby, sordid place, and Madame a comical figure with clownish make-up and a bizarre wig.

The Whichart girls are also seen in a very different light from the innocent, talented Fossils. Maimie (Pauline) becomes a chorus girl at

15 and by 16 has started an affair with an influential producer. Daisy (Posy) gives up her dancing career and ends up in respectable suburbia with her rediscovered grandparents. Noel allows only Tania (Petrova) a satisfying ending. She finds her mother and goes off with her for a year's exotic travel, with the future promise of an aeroplane. There seems a very clear message that the stage is not a worthy career choice, Noel's own experiences clearly still influencing her.

The Whicharts seems too brittle, too cynical, too determined to shock. *Ballet Shoes*, on the other hand, has an inner truth, a sweetness that never becomes sentimental, a moral message that hard work and talent and belief in yourself can sometimes make your dreams come true. It was the best two shillings I ever spent.

JACQUELINE WILSON has written over a hundred books for children. The main character in her book about evacuees, *Wave Me Goodbye*, fantasizes that she is a fourth Fossil sister. Jacqueline has actually achieved her acting ambition: she has a cameo role in a forthcoming film adaptation of her book *Four Children and It*.

Word Magic

TIM MACKINTOSH-SMITH

Are writers born or bred? One of my grandfathers was a poet — an exact contemporary of Kipling, though rather less famous. His main contribution to literature was the invention of the poetry postcard. He also invented 'The Quick and Easy Method of Washing Floors', that ingenious bucket with a pedal that presses two rollers together and squeezes your mop, and which is found in every school and hospital throughout the universe; he sold the rights to it for, I think, twenty guineas. I'm sure I've inherited his lack of business acumen. Perhaps I've also inherited his way with words. But if there is indeed such a thing as a literary gene, I don't believe it's yet been mapped.

I can, however, map the beginnings of my path to writerhood, the nurture rather than the nature. First, there's me lying in a cot in a bow window, listening to a blackbird singing in the silver birch, and to my father and his friends playing string quartets in the room below (probably Haydn, and jolly, though they had their darker moments). In my memory, music comes before words. But words come early, too, together with images. There I am again, still in the mewling and puking phase, being wheeled along the road to see my favourite image, the Esso Tiger.

PUT A TIGER IN YOUR TANK!

my mother would say, reading the slogan on the giant hoarding. Then one day she recited,

> Tyger Tyger, burning bright,
> In the forests of the night . . .

The words came like a spell. The Tyger devoured 'This Little Piggy' and all its feeble peers; or nearly all, for there could still be poetry in the nursery rhyme:

> Hark, hark, the dogs do bark:
> The beggars are coming to town . . .

thrilled me, and still does.

More thrilling still was Matins, which we attended every Sunday in 'the fairest, goodliest, and most famous parish church in England', as Queen Elizabeth I justly called it. Columns, chords and words soared and burst far above in vaulting and echoes. Best of all were those Sundays when my big brothers, beruffed and deceptively angelic, sang the *Benedicite*. I loved the way it went through the gamut of creation from angels to whales, and ended,

> O Ananias, Azarias, and Misael, bless ye the Lord:
> praise him and magnify him for ever.

I was never quite sure who or what those three were, but their names were magic to my ears.

Words, music and magic interwove. At home, my growing life began to revolve around a piano. Life did, necessarily, for us all: the piano was a concert grand, the elephant in the room. But it was a lovable monster, a member of the family. I spent many happy hours sitting under it (a sign of an artistic bent in children, Jan Morris says). I'm looking now at a photograph of us four siblings with the great beast: my sister at the keyboard; my brothers with guitar and trumpet; me, aged 3, bashing a tin drum with grim concentration – and a disturbing resemblance to weird little Oskar in Günter Grass's *Die Blechtrommel* . . . That orotund German word brings me back to why the piano came to mind. It had brass letters on the inside of the lid, and some of my earliest stabs at reading were attempts to decipher them. When I finally did make them out, they seemed to have no meaning:

HERMANN WAGNER STUTTGART

'It's the piano's name,' my father explained. And the way he pronounced it, with Teutonic vowels and growls — '*Hairrghmaan Vaagnairrgh Shtootgaarrght*' – sounded absolutely right for that mahogany mammoth. (Poor Hermann: we eventually all but killed him with Dvorak's *Slavonic Dances*, played *fff*, sometimes the whole quartet of us pounding away together at once. He's now enjoying a well-earned retirement in a Chinese community centre, if he hasn't been bored to death by woodworm or by endless performances of 'Chopsticks'.)

Then, suddenly, letters and meaning came together. I was in bed with *Alice*, and can remember the moment: the Tenniel picture of the White Rabbit, the words that went with it –

> Oh my ears and w-w wh . . .
> And *whiskies*? No,
> and *whiskers*

– and the rapturous realization: I could read!

Music, meaning, magic, letters now began to coalesce, and soon to issue – in verse – from my infant pen: 'The lions in the jungle', went one effort, perhaps subliminally inspired by Blake's 'Tyger',

John Tenniel

> Have a huge great roar,
> And little things that pass by night
> Are frightened of their snore.

There would be no looking back.

A few years on, at the age of 9, the roaring of lions and tygers accompanied my first ventures into Latin. My school was next door to a zoo, and Mr Hutchinson's classroom was filled with verbs, nouns and safari sounds. 'The subject goes in the nominative,' we chanted, to a background of bestial howls and grunts,

> The object goes in the accusative,
> Genitive 'of',
> Dative 'to' or 'for',
> Ablative 'by', 'with' or 'from' –
> POM-POM!

'That's it, boys, never forget the "*Pom-pom!*"' (An elephant trumpeted agreement.) Mr Hutchinson had longish grey hair, and a faint resemblance to the first Dr Who, the television Time Lord.

It was Mr Hutchinson who gave me the final, fateful push down the path to writing. Along with Latin, he taught us English. In Latin I did well; in English I starred, together with a boy called Snowy Owen. (Snowy, where are you now? Is your hair still that same ashen alien blond? Or has it gone to dust and ashes like mine?) I can remember none of my rival's productions; but fragments of one of mine have survived, from a poem entitled 'Agincourt'. Miniature fogey and ghastly swot, I declaimed unblushing to the class,

> The English army, lo! it sought
> The way that led to Agincourt . . .

Down in the zoo, a gibbon gibbered. I ignored my classmates' giggles and continued. There were some good bits coming:

> Then, Twang! the bowstrings go again –
> The sky is filled with arrow-rain.

We were in the era of *Howl*, *The Naked Lunch* and 'Lucy in the Sky with Diamonds'. But Mr Hutchinson's literary taste transcended time and trend, for he awarded me twenty-five marks out of twenty for my prodigious anachronism. With that sort of encouragement, how could I *not* have become a writer?

*

Not long ago, on the Internet, another series of word-and-memory associations (for that is all that these paragraphs have been) led me to the news that Mr Hutchinson had died in his ninetieth year. I hadn't seen him for the best part of half a century, and – to be honest – had hardly thought of him; I'd had other teachers who were more flamboyant, more eccentric, even more memorable. And yet I felt the loss, and still do.

I needn't. Mr Hutchinson *is* a Time Lord. We all have some gift of the Spirit, some spark of Promethean fire, and teachers like him find it, fan it into flame,

> *Et quasi cursores vitaï lampada tradunt*
> And, like runners, relay the torch of life

– as he himself might have quoted, if we'd ever got as far as Lucretius. Great teachers relay genius as parents pass on genes. They all transcend time.

But no one else has ever given me twenty-five out of twenty, and no one ever will.

TIM MACKINTOSH-SMITH has spent the past four years pinned down by conflict in his adoptive land, Yemen. He has, however, been writing to the roar of missiles, not least a 3,000-year Arab history (*The Arab Story*, Yale University Press). His article was first published in the Emirates Airline Festival of Literature's anthology *For the Love of Words*.

Bibliography

Field Marshal Lord Alanbrooke, *War Diaries, 1939–1945* 69

Noel Annan, *Our Age* 44

Edmund Crispin, *The Case of the Gilded Fly*; *Holy Disorders*;
The Moving Toyshop; *Swan Song*; *Love Lies Bleeding*; *Buried for
Pleasure*; *Frequent Hearses*; *The Long Divorce*; *The Glimpses of
the Moon* 77

Roald Dahl, *Boy* 15

Peter Davidson, *The Last of the Light* 63

Penelope Fitzgerald, *The Means of Escape* 21

Tim Mackintosh-Smith: on becoming a writer 89

F. M. McNeill, *The Scots Kitchen* 40

Olivia Manning, The Balkan trilogy: *The Great Fortune*; *The Spoilt
City*; *Friends and Heroes* 7

Dorothy L. Sayers, *Gaudy Night* 49

Noel Streatfeild, *Ballet Shoes*; *The Whicharts* 83

Jan Struther: the poetry of 55

Rosemary Sutcliff, *The Eagle of the Ninth*; *The Silver Branch* 33

Alfred, Lord Tennyson, *In Memoriam* 26

Coming attractions

EDMUND GORDON fetches up at Henry Green's party ·
DAISY HAY accepts Joyce Grenfell's invitation · HENRY
JEFFREYS props up the bar with Kingsley Amis · LAURIE
GRAHAM prepares for a Cradock-style Christmas · TIM PEARS
finds family history in a Polish forest · MELISSA HARRISON
learns to see through the rhetoric · CHARLES ELLIOTT enjoys
some eighteenth-century gossip · KATE YOUNG picnics at
Hanging Rock · PAUL BRASSLEY meets a legendary journalist ·
MARY HELEN SPOONER attends an unusual
cremation

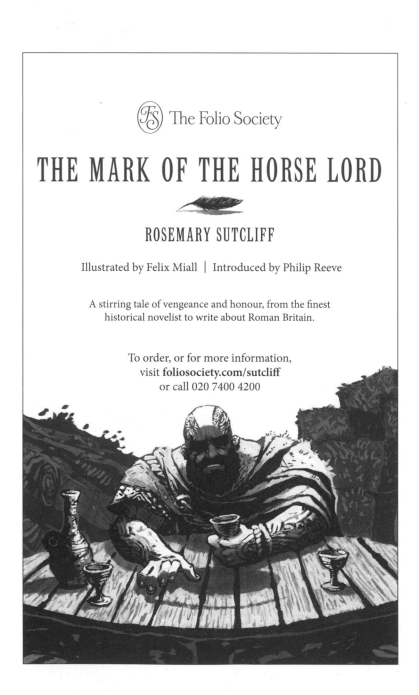

The Folio Society

THE MARK OF THE HORSE LORD

ROSEMARY SUTCLIFF

Illustrated by Felix Miall | Introduced by Philip Reeve

A stirring tale of vengeance and honour, from the finest
historical novelist to write about Roman Britain.

To order, or for more information,
visit **foliosociety.com/sutcliff**
or call 020 7400 4200